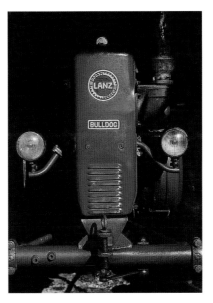

CLASSIC
TRACTORS
of the WORLD

By Nick Baldwin

Photographs by
Andrew Morland

Foreword by
Harold L. Brock,
Ford and John Deere
Tractor Designer

Voyageur Press
A TOWN SQUARE BOOK

Edited by Michael Dregni
Designed by Andrea Rud
Printed in Hong Kong

98 99 00 01 02   5 4 3 2 1

Library of Congress Cataloging-in-Publication Data
Baldwin, Nick.
    Classic tractors of the world / Nick Baldwin.
      p. cm.
    Includes index.
    ISBN 0-89658-394-5
    1. Farm tractors. I. Title.
    TL233.B255 1998
    629.225'2—dc21   98-2944
                        CIP

A Town Square Book
published by Voyageur Press, Inc.
123 North Second Street, P.O. Box 338, Stillwater, MN 55082 U.S.A.
651-430-2210, fax 651-430-2211

Distributed in Europe by Midland Publishing Ltd.
Unit 3, Maizefield, Hinckley Fields, Leicester LE10 1YF, England
Tel: 01455 233 747, Fax: 01455 233 737, E-mail: midlandbooks@compuserve.com

Educators, fundraisers, premium and gift buyers, publicists, and marketing managers: Looking for creative products and new sales ideas? Voyageur Press books are available at special discounts when purchased in quantities, and special editions can be created to your specifications. For details contact the marketing department at 800-888-9653.

Page 1, top row, left to right: *1939 Massey-Harris Super 101; 1954 Lanz Bulldog D 2806; Le Percheron.* Bottom row, left to right: *Late-1960s SAME 480DTB; 1919 Case Crossmotor; 1955 MAN AS440H*
Page 2: *1954 McCormick-Deering Farmall Super MD-TA. Owner: Donald Schaeffer of Grabill, Indiana, USA.*
Page 3: *1930 Mercedes-Benz tractor catalog cover art.*

ACKNOWLEDGMENTS

Many thanks to all the enthusiastic owners of the tractors photographed for this book, many of whom helped us despite the language barriers. Happily, our common enthusiasm for the tractors broke down most of the problems. Thanks for all their time, great hospitality, and cooperation, without which completing such a book would be impossible. Our thanks to: Cory Nijsen; Jud Puttern; Marinus Koppens; Jacques Monnerat; Marc Solvet; Hank Van Doorn; Frans Nouwen; Pedro VD Burget; Michel Jaeken; Janet Peters; Christian Denis; Jan Nijssen; W. VD Putten; Harry Wilms; Basrt, Theo, and Johan Sauwen; Lucien Delaroque; Daniel and Nelly Binet; Yoann Binet and Caroline Boullot; Charles, Nathalie, and Anne Hingant; Christian Anxe; Jean-Claude Cardine; Paul Hembury; Jim Thomas; Aubrey Sanders; David Hunt; Mike Broom; Pierre Bouillé; W. Laarakkers; D. and J. Symington; Don Wolf; Arland Lepper; Kenneth Anderson; Wendell Lampson; Palmer Fossum; Norm Seveik; J. R. Gyger; Sue Dougan; Eric Coates; Dennis Crossman; Jonathan Philp; Duke Potter; Jim Spark; Ivan Sparks; Brian Whitlock; Clarence DeLacour; Paul Cluyas; Jim Grant; the Schaefer Family; Peter and Mike Fletcher; Gruber Jurgen; Malcolm Goddard; Christopher Shere; the Aigner Family; Tom and Cindy Armstrong of N-Complete; Floyd Dominque; Mike Hanna; Dean Simmons; and the late Charles Cawood and Fritz Nischwitz.

Many thanks to Bob Wright and the Ford Motor Company for providing a Mondeo and a Taurus Station Wagon, both of which made the many thousands of miles of motoring a pleasure.

Thanks to John Deere at Mannheim; Leo "Lanz" Speer and his fascinating Lanz Museum at Mitterrohrbach in southern Germany; the Museum of English Rural Life at University of Reading, Great Britain; the Farm Museum at Milton, Ontario, Canada; the Historisch Festival at Panningen, the Netherlands, an event run by the Historische Moteren en Traktoren Vereniging every year during the last weekend of July; the Great Dorset Steam Fair, near Blandford, Dorset, Great Britain, an annual event at the end of August; La Locomotion en Fête, held at Cerny La Ferte Alais, France, every year; the Western Minnesota Steam Threshers Reunion at Rollag, Minnesota, held every Labor Day; Tractomania each Autumn near Toulouse, France; Centre Historique de L'Agriculture, Moulin de Chiblins, Switzerland; and Ferg Innes, Booleroo Steam and Traction Preservation Society, Booleroo, South Australia, which holds a big event each March.

Finally, thanks to Peter Love of *Tractors and Machinery* magazine, Cudham, Kent, Great Britain.

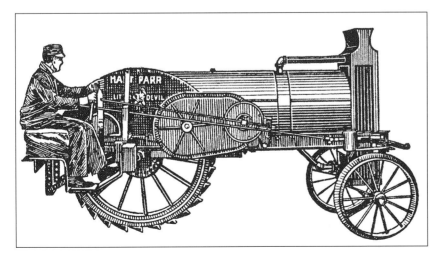

1910s Hart-Parr Little Devil tractor advertisement art.

CONTENTS

1940s Deere Model H

1954 Lanz B Bulldog D 2806

1921 Renault HO

Fordson advertisement

Case brochure

1930s McCormick-Deering WD-40

FOREWORD

By Harold L. Brock
Ford N Series tractor design engineer 1939–1958
Deere & Company New Generation tractor engineering executive 1959–1985
Society of Automotive Engineers president 1971

Having been involved with the design and development of farm tractors beginning with the Ford 9N of 1939 through the era of John Deere's New Generation of tractors, launched in 1960, I read with great interest Nick Baldwin and Andrew Morland's compilation of the innumerable attempts to mechanize farming throughout the world.

I am astounded by the great proliferation of farm tractor designs that existed to accomplish the replacement of animal power on the world's farms. The many variables of crops, topography, weather, cropping practices, and more, resulted in the development of many unique configurations of tractors to work in local conditions. No single "worldwide" tractor design evolved from these many attempts; instead, many countries had their own particular models that they believed were most appropriate for their marketplace and style of agriculture.

At the dawn of the twentieth century, farmers in Europe and North America sought machines to replace animal power, and numerous inventors, engineers, and designers increased their efforts to meet this challenge. During World War I, it was recognized that greater emphasis should be put on the mechanized production of food with less reliance on manual and animal power; efforts by the Ford Motor Company resulted in the introduction of the famous Fordson tractor. With the demand for more farm tractors, other tractor companies around the globe also introduced a variety of lightweight models copying these basic early designs.

As new models of tractors were developed during the 1920s, the adaptation of mounted equipment in addition to pull-behind equipment became more important. Unfortunately, most equipment was not interchangeable between competitive tractors, thus requiring the purchaser to buy new equipment when changing makes of tractors. However, the configurations and features of the major tractor makers became more common.

My mentor, Henry Ford Sr. recognized the great need to replace the some 17,000,000 horses and mules still being used on North American farms in 1939; he believed the farmer needed a tractor that would do all the chores that animals performed. Mr. Ford's famous Handshake Agreement with Irishman Harry Ferguson to design and produce a tractor incorporating Ferguson's three-point hitch was envisioned to accomplish this objective. Mr. Ford asked that I be made project manager for this new tractor. His charge to me was that the tractor should be completely new and should not cost the consumer more than a team of animals, their harness, and the cost of 10 acres (4 hectares) of land to feed them. He firmly believed if we could accomplish this objective, the farm tractor would be a worthwhile investment for the farmer. In addition, the tractor would free up more land for production of food crops to feed the world.

Working with Mr. Ford convinced me that he was a great visionary with little interest in the profitability of projects. He challenged our small group to accomplish for the farm community what he had accomplished for transportation with the inexpensive Ford Model T automobile. I am delighted to observe that some fifty-seven years after the debut of the Ford 9N tractor, Mr. Ford's objective has accomplished its purpose. The utility tractor concept has evolved, and the principles of this design have been incorporated in almost all tractors produced in the worldwide market today. With the adoption of the three-point hitch on all tractors, the farmer now has the advantage of adapting equipment to a standard hitch configuration.

This book reflects the evolution of farm tractors throughout the world, illuminating Henry Ford's quest to, as he himself said, take the burden of farming from flesh and blood and put it on steel.

AUSTRALIA

Australia is one of the world's great agricultural nations, and it is thus little surprise that the country has also been home to several prolific builders of farm tractors.

The country has a long and varied history of producing tractors. The firms of A. H. McDonald and Caldwell Vale were tractor pioneers in Australia with histories dating back to the 1900s and 1910s; others such as Cliff Howard and Frank Jelbart built tractors in the 1920s. In recent years, several massive four-wheel-drive prairie types have been created by Waltanna, Upton, Baldwin, Phillips, Acremaster, and others.

1950s Chamberlain 40K
Facing page: *From the first tractor released in 1949 to the end of the run in 1955, only about 2,000 of Bob Chamberlain's famous 40K and 40KA tractors were sold during the model's production life.*

Facing page: **Chamberlain 40K and 40KA advertisement.**

Through the years, there has also been major investment in the Australian market from the large multinational firms, with International Harvester in particular represented by a large factory in Australia dating back to 1938.

CALDWELL VALE

In 1907, brothers Felix and Norman Caldwell crafted an incredible tractor prototype that boasted features far ahead of its time, including four-wheel drive, four-wheel power-assisted steering, and a crude but pioneering implement lift. With backing from Sydney financier Henry Vale, the Caldwell Vale Motor & Tractor Construction Company of Auburn, New South Wales, went into tractor production in 1910, building 30- to 80-horsepower tractors and trucks with four-wheel drive. Some Caldwell Vale models had mid-mounted disc plows while others featured four-wheel steering. However, all were too heavy and expensive to have widespread appeal, and despite the 1913 creation of a four-wheel-drive, four-wheel-steering touring car, the business soon foundered.

CHAMBERLAIN

Bob Chamberlain was a tractor mechanic in Western Australia in the 1930s. After fixing more than his share of broken-down machines, he reckoned he could build a better tractor. Chamberlain believed that extra power and nine gears would increase cultivation speed, so in 1945, he created a tractor prototype propelled by a horizontally opposed, two-cylinder, kerosene-powered engine that developed 40 horsepower.

In 1949, Chamberlain Industries Ltd. of Welshpool began production of its Model 40K. Some 2,000 40K tractors were built, as well as a small number of more powerful types with 60- and 70-horsepower Detroit diesels. A larger, diesel-powered Model DA was also created from the two-cylinder K.

In 1955, Chamberlain released a less-expensive Champion model with a Perkins 45-horsepower diesel engine. A Champion with suitable gearing to give it a top speed of 65 miles per hour (104 km/h) successfully joined in several car endurance rallies, culminating in an 11,000-mile (17,600-km) dash around Australia in 1957.

In 1970, John Deere took a 49 percent stake in Chamberlain, and soon Deere components were being used in Chamberlain tractors. Chamberlain continued to build its own models powered by Deere engines up to 1986.

1950s Chamberlain 40K

During World War II, Bob Chamberlain designed tanks in the United States. After the war, he returned to Australia and began work developing his 40K tractor. The prototype was built at the Rolloy Piston Company run by his family, and was first field tested at the end of 1945. Although developed in Melbourne, the 40K actually entered production in 1949 thousands of miles away at a munitions factory in Perth, Western Australia. Owner: Aubrey Sanders.

1950s Chamberlain Champion

Left: *The mid-1950s Chamberlain Champion was designed to complete with the less-expensive imported tractors that were invading the Australian market after World War II. The Champion was powered by a 45-horsepower Perkins four-cylinder diesel.*

1930s Howard DH22 with Rotary Hoe

Below: *The Howard DH22 was designed to power the Howard Rotavator. The tractor began production in the 1930s with a Morris 22-horsepower engine and then gained more powerful American engines, culminating in a 35-horsepower Le Roi.*

Howard

Arthur Clifford "Cliff" Howard invented his Rotavator rotary cultivator in 1914, but there were so few tractors available to power the novel implement that Howard was not able to build complete machines until years later. In 1923, he established Austral Auto Cultivators Ltd. in Moss Vale, New South Wales, and began production of his self-propelled three-wheel machine. Howard's tractors soon ranged from 60-horsepower four-wheelers down to 5-, 8-, and 12-horsepower pedestrian-controlled models.

With the arrival of the Fordson, Howard created a special rotary cultivator for the ubiquitous lightweight tractor. A 16-horsepower Morris-powered Howard three-wheel tractor was also made in the late 1920s. In the early 1930s, Morris 22-horsepower engines propelled Howard DH four-wheelers with lower gearing than conventional tractors for "rotavation."

In 1938, Cliff Howard switched his attention to Britain, creating Rotary Hoe Cultivators Ltd. in Essex. The firm built Rotary Hoes and the short-lived Platypus crawler of the 1950s. Four-wheelers continued in Australia, including 35-horsepower Le Roi–engined two- and four-wheel-drive types in the 1950s. Since the 1960s, the firm has made smaller, Briggs & Stratton–engined models for horticultural and yard purposes.

Jelbart

Frank Jelbart of Ballarat, Victoria, made some of Australia's first stationary engines in the early years of the century. In 1914, Jelbart was fitting his engines to Jelbart tractors, which remained in production for about ten years.

McDonald

The tractor pioneer of Australia is Alfred Henry McDonald's A. H. McDonald & Company of Melbourne. In 1908, McDonald built its first tractor, the Imperial EA Type All Steel Oil Tractor, powered by a 20-horsepower two-cylinder engine; it was first sold in 1909.

McDonald continued building tractors into the 1920s until less-expensive imports made it imperative that the firm import Swedish Avance and American Emerson-Brantingham machines instead.

After an absence from manufacturing of ten years, McDonald returned to tractor production in 1929, initially using a Rumely OilPull frame with the firm's own indirect-injection Super Diesel engine. Soon, McDonald built the whole tractor, and more than 600 were sold before World War II disrupted output.

Following the war, McDonald resumed limited production up to 1955 with more-powerful, 40-horsepower two-stroke engines.

Ronaldson Bros & Tippett

David and Adam Ronaldson and Jack Tippett's Ronaldson Bros & Tippett of Ballarat, Victoria, had made a hundred portable and stationary engines by 1908, and built a tractor prototype soon afterward. However, it was not until the mid-1920s that the firm began series production of tractors, building the Ronaldson Tippett Super Drive, a licensed version of the Illinois Tractor Company's Super Drive from Bloomington, Illinois. The Australian version used imported American parts, including 30-horsepower Wisconsin engines. These Super Drives lasted through to the late 1930s, after which engines alone were built. The firm remained a licensed maker and importer of Wisconsin engines until 1972.

Sunshine

The famous Sunshine Harvester Works of Braybrook Junction, Melbourne, South Australia, also manufactured a tractor as self-propulsion became a priority during World War I. American Continental engines were used, and some Sunshines featured conventional truck-type radiators while others had horizontal drums made out of dozens of pipes plumbed into circular ends. Sunshine production ended in the 1920s.

CANADA

Canada, one of the world's great grain-producing nations, often used "Canadian Special" versions of American tractors in the early days of the agricultural machinery market. Examples include the Northwest steam traction engine made in the early 1900s by the Northwest Thresher Company of Stillwater, Minnesota, which was relabeled and sold into Canada by the American-Abell Engine & Threshing Company of Toronto, Ontario. Northwest's Universal gas tractor was later built and sold by the Hero Manufacturing Company of Winnipeg, Manitoba, in the 1910s. Similarly, the American-market Illinois Super-Drive tractor from the Illinois Tractor Company of Bloomington, Illinois, was imported into Canada as the Imperial Super-Drive by the Robert Bell Engine & Thresher Company of Seaforth, Ontario.

1939 Massey-Harris Super 101
Facing page: *A Chrysler-powered Super 101 with Lavon Fred of Fred Farms, Indiana, USA, at the wheel.*

1930s Massey-Harris General Purpose
Above: *Mass-produced four-wheel-drive tractors were a rarity when the 22-horsepower General Purpose first appeared in the early 1930s. The model had rigidly attached front axles but the rear axle was free to pivot. It was revised in 1936 with a more powerful engine.*

1910s Sawyer-Massey 11/22

The Sawyer-Massey Company of Hamilton, Ontario, became an important producer of Canadian steam traction engines after the Massey family of Massey-Harris fame took a minority interest in the firm in 1892. Gas tractors were built from 1910, including this two-speed 11/22 dating from the end of World War I. Owner: Jacques Monneral of Boissy-le-Chatel, France.

Several Canadian entrepreneurs soon embarked on building their own models. The Sawyer-Massey Company of Hamilton, Ontario, was one of the main Canadian steam and gasoline tractor builders from the 1860s through the 1920s, competing with the other major pioneering Canadian manufacturer, Goold, Shapley & Muir Company of Brantford, Ontario. Other small tractor makers included the Canadian tractor built in 1919 by the Alberta Foundry & Machine Company of Medicine Hat, Alberta; the 1918 Rein Drive from the Rein Drive Tractor Company of Toronto, Ontario; the 1916 Sterling made by the Sterling Engine Works of Winnipeg, Manitoba; and the 1915 One Man Motor Plow from the Savoie-Guay Company of Plessisville, Quebec. Other makers built licensed versions of British tractors. During World War II, many Canadian-built tractors from famous American companies were sold into Great Britain because of Dominion tax advantages.

COCKSHUTT

James G. Cockshutt's Cockshutt Plow Company of Brantford, Ontario, made plows starting in 1877. In the 1930s, it added a range of implements as well as tractors built for the firm by Oliver Hart-Parr. In 1946, Cockshutt's Bellevue, Ohio, plant introduced the Buda-engined Cockshutt 30 that was also sold in the United States as the Co-op E-3 by the National Farm Machinery Cooperative of Bellevue and as the Farmcrest, sold through the famous American Gambles Stores chain.

In 1947, Cockshutt came up with a "live" power takeoff (PTO) with a shaft that continued to revolve even when the clutch was disengaged; the PTO design was widely copied. Models with larger Continental and Hercules engines followed from Ohio and Ontario, although as diesels increased in popularity, Perkins became a popular engine choice.

In 1962, White bought Cockshutt, and tractors continued to be made for only a short while longer.

1938 Cockshutt 80

The Cockshutt 80 was in fact the good old three-plow Oliver 80 painted in Cockshutt's colors. This was appropriate in view of Cockshutt's eventual acquisition by Oliver as part of the White group. The Cockshutt 80 did a good job of hiding its Oliver identity, and one wonders how many farmers realized what they were buying. Owners: Keller Family of Forest Junction, Wisconsin, USA.

1950s Cockshutt 50 Diesel
Above: *The Cockshutt 50 Diesel was offered from 1953 to 1957 and used a Buda six-cylinder 273-ci (4.47-liter) engine with a five-speed transmission.*

1950 Cockshutt 30
Left: *The Cockshutt 30 was powered by a Buda four-cylinder valve-in-head 153-ci (2.5-liter) engine available in diesel, gas, distillate, or propane forms. The same tractor was available in the United States as the Co-op E-3. This tractor is on display at the Ontario Agricultural Museum of Milton, Ontario.*

MASSEY-HARRIS AND MASSEY-FERGUSON

The Massey-Harris Company of Toronto, Ontario, was formed in 1891 by the merger of the Massey Manufacturing Company of Toronto and A. Harris, Son & Company of Brantford, Ontario. The new firm wisely left the infant tractor business to others and did not become seriously involved until World War I, and then only with other firms' designs—first the Bull tractor, and then the Parrett from the Parrett Tractor Company of Chicago, Illinois.

In 1928, Massey bought the J. I. Case Plow Works of Racine, Wisconsin, acquiring the Wallis tractor in the process. Jerome Increase Case founded both the Case Plow Works and the J. I. Case Threshing Machine Company, which made Case tractors, but the two firms had no other corporate link until they were united in 1929 minus the Wallis interests. The advanced Wallis tractors had been sold by M-H since 1927, and now became the basis for a new range, which also came to include a trend-setting 15/22 General Purpose tractor

with four-wheel drive by four equal-sized wheels.

Late 1930s advances included the Twin-Power tractors with two governor settings and four- and six-cylinder proprietary engines from Chrysler and others.

In 1953, Massey-Harris took over Irishman Harry Ferguson's tractor business, which had prospered in England since his falling out with Ford. This led to the demise of the little M-H Pony, which had become popular in Canada and France. All the tractors were soon re-badged Massey-Ferguson, and with the take-over of the Perkins engine business in 1958–1959, the firm became one of the first in North America to offer a complete range of diesel tractors.

Massey-Ferguson was later bought by the Varity Corporation, and was subsequently purchased by the Allis-Gleaner Company (AGCO) in 1994.

VERSATILE

The Versatile Manufacturing Company of Winnipeg, Manitoba, built massive, four-wheel-drive tractors starting in 1966. Versatiles were sold in Europe by Fiat from 1979 and in Australia by Ford. In 1987, Ford acquired Versatile.

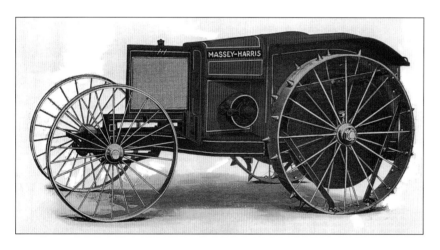

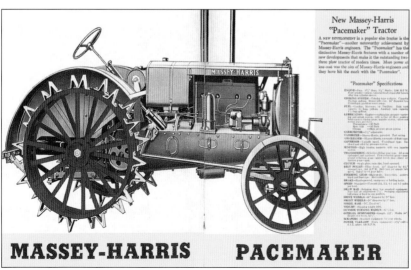

1920s Massey-Harris No. 2
Left, top: *Massey-Harris's No. 1 tractor was the American Bull model. The Canadian giant's No. 2 tractor was designed by the Parrett Tractor Company and was offered with a Buda 12/22 engine for several years in the late 1910s and early 1920s.*

1930s Massey-Harris Pacemaker
Left, bottom: *The mid-1930s Pacemaker was evolved from the first unit-frame Wallis-based Massey-Harris tractor.*

1949 Massey-Harris Pony
Facing page: *The one-plow Pony was built in large numbers in both France and Canada.*

1942 Massey Harris 81R
Above: *The 81R was one of Massey-Harris's 81 range that was built from 1941 to 1948 with a break in production in 1943. The tractor was propelled by a 124-ci (2.1-liter) Continental engine.*

1950 Massey-Harris Model 22
Right: *The Model 22 was available from 1949 as an RT row-crop or STD standard model. Power came from a Continental 18/27-horsepower engine, and the tractor featured the Depth-O-Matic hydraulic linkage.*

FRANCE

F rance was one of the pioneers of successful light cars, so French manufacturers should have been in a good position to mechanize the country's agriculture. However, French farms were small and farmers were on average poor, so despite important tractor trials at Bourges in 1912 and Senlis in 1919, sales of the early tractors were slow.

French tractor engineers had many novel engineering concepts, such as Tourand-Latil's hydraulic implement lift and Auror's four-wheel-drive system, both from the 1920s; by the 1930s, diesels became widespread. Still, only 27,000 tractors were in use in France in 1929, and this figure increased by only 2,000 more tractors over the next decade.

The great boom in mechanized farming in France came after World War II, and the number of tractors at work on French farms reached 700,000 by 1959. Interestingly, only 4,500 new diesel tractors were registered in 1956, a figure that skyrocketed to 23,500 a year later.

1927 Renault PE
Facing page: *Renault's PE model tractor was powered by a 14-horsepower engine that was derived from one of Renault's automobiles.*

Above: **Renault tractor catalog art.**

Despite the pre-eminence of Renault, foreign tractors provided the greatest impetus to mechanize French farm production. American tractor firms sold 40,000 machines in France in the years 1945–1960, compared with 52,500 from Britain and almost 70,000 from Germany.

In addition to importing tractors, many foreign firms set up factories in France. Austin of England became a major producer in France between the wars. After World War II, International Harvester, Massey-Harris (later Massey-Ferguson), and Minneapolis-Moline (made in France by the car firm Mathis of Strasbourg) all set the pace—even if Allis-Chalmers's work with Vendeuvre and Case's involvement with SFV later proved disastrous. Renault's links with German, and recently German-American, manufacturers has proved to be far more successful.

The best known of the tractors made by outsiders in France was the Massey-Harris Pony. Introduced in 1948 and made at Marquette-lez-Lille, Nord, from 1951, the 25,000th Pony was built in late 1954. The Massey-Harris Pony, along with the Ferguson, probably did more to revolutionize French agriculture than any other models.

1953 Massey-Harris Pony French brochure
Left: *The Massey-Harris Pony graced the cover of this 1953 French brochure. Production of the Pony began at Massey-Harris's factory at Marquette-lez-Lille (Nord) in 1951, and 25,000 Ponies had been built by 1955.*

1950s Ferguson TEF-20
Facing page: *By the 1950s, the French Hotchkiss firm was ending its days as a car maker, but the venerable company still built trucks and tractors, producing Jeeps and Fergusons under license. This Ferguson TEF-20 is one of approximately 7,000 Ferguson tractors made in France. Owner: Michel Jaeken of Bocholt, Belgium.*

1919 RIP

Above: *The French 1919 RIP was based on the Heider tractor from the American Rock Island Plow Company—hence the acronym RIP. It was powered by a 20-horsepower Waukesha engine. RIP went on to make quite different machines with CLM diesels, culminating in a Mercedes-Benz–powered model in 1939. Owner: Jacques Monneral of Boissy-le-Chatel, France.*

1918 SCEMIA U-20

Left: *The SCEMIA U-20 was a British Saunderson Universal in all but name. SCEMIA (Société de Construction et d'Entretien de Matériel Industriel et Agricole) made tractors as well as buses. This U-20 featured a 15/25-horsepower Schneider engine. Owner: Marc Solvet of Meaux, France.*

1950s International Farmall Cub

From early on, International tractors were sold in France by CIMA (Compagne Internationale des Machines Agricoles). IHC later opened factories at Croix (Nord) and Monataire (Oise) and built roughly 100,000 tractors in France from 1951 to 1961. CIMA's initials appear on this early French-built Cub.

CITROËN

André Citroën's famous firm briefly experimented with tractor prototypes in the late 1910s and early 1920s, but after building a few hundred small machines around 1920, Citroën halted tractor production. The firm built another tractor prototype in the 1940s before divesting from the agricultural market.

1919 Citroën

Citroën made a brief foray into the tractor field at the end of World War I, and about only 700 of this 1919 Citroën tractor were built. The tractor was based on a Citroën automobile and retained the car's 5-horsepower engine, but featured unit construction. In the early stages of World War II, Citroën returned to the tractor field with an experimental four-wheel drive.

LABOURIER

Located high in the Jura Mountains at Mouchard, Labourier started in the 1920s by converting ex–World War I trucks from the Four Wheel Drive Company (FWD) of Wisconsin for snow-plow, haulage, and forestry duties. These conversions gradually evolved into a make in their own right, and in 1941, light agricultural models were added as well as larger four-wheel drives similar to the French Latil tractors.

Monsieur Labourier was lying in a hospital bed in about 1930 when he had heard a diesel airplane pass overhead. He was so impressed that he traced the maker of the opposed-piston two-stroke to the French firm Compagnie Lilloise des Moteurs (CLM), which built German Junkers-licensed engines, and employed many smaller versions of the CLM engine in his trucks and tractors. Labourier machines were later powered by engines from other makers, including Alsthom, Peugeot, Perkins, and Berliet.

From the 1920s into the 1970s, Labourier built about 15,000 tractors, including high-clearance vineyard models and a few combine harvesters. After the 1970s, competition became too intense in the tractor field, and Labourier concentrated on making spare parts and gears for other manufacturers.

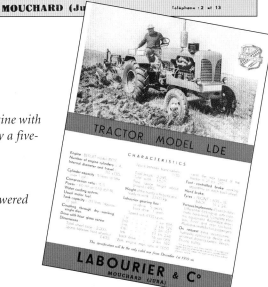

1940s Labourier LD 25
Above: *Labourier's LD 25 was propelled by a CLM two-cylinder diesel engine with four opposed pistons. The CLM created 25 horsepower and was backed by a five-speed gearbox.*

1959 Labourier LDE
Right: *A British brochure for Labourier's LDE of 1959. The tractor was powered by a Berliet 305-ci (5.0-liter) engine.*

1952 Labourier LD 15
Above: *The LD 15 had a single-cylinder, twin-piston CLM 15-horsepower diesel made by a subsidiary of Peugeot under Junkers license. The gearbox featured five forward speeds.*

1952 Labourier LD 15
Right: *From its small factory in the Jura region, Labourier made a wide assortment of tractors in the 1950s, including this 1952 LD15. Owner: H. Potelle of Méru, France.*

LATIL AND TOURAND-LATIL

In 1898, Georges Latil devised a front-wheel-driven engine pack in Marseilles that could replace horses in the shafts of all manner of carts, carriages, and implements. In 1914, he perfected a four-wheel-drive tractor with four-wheel steering that was widely used for military purposes, and after World War I, became the basis of many agricultural machines built by a variety of different French firms. Several models were made by Tourand, who also offered a three-wheeler in the 1920s with single roller drive at the rear and one of the earliest hydraulic power lifts. The Latil four-wheel drives were expensive machines suitable for contractors and the largest farms. In the 1930s, Latils were also built in Belgium and England.

During World War II, MAN of Germany took control of Latil's Paris factory to build war materiel.

Following World War II, Latils were primarily used for haulage and forestry purposes, and they continued to be built in England even after Renault's acquisition of the French original in 1955.

Latil later became part of the French Société Anonyme de Véhicules Industriels et Équipements Mécaniques (SAVIEM) group, which also included the Société d'Outillage Mécanique et d'Usinage Artillerie (SOMUA), maker of cultivators and horticultural tractors. Under SAVIEM, Latil ceased to take an interest in the farm market, although the firm continued to build four-wheel-drive forestry tractors, even after Brimont of France took control in 1974. Brimont later returned to its own specialty of farm trailers.

1934 Latil JTL
Latil's JTL featured a 183-ci (3.0-liter) gasoline engine and six forward gears. It could turn five furrows thanks to its four-wheel drive and the various types of cleated wheels that were available. As this brochure noted, the JTL "Remplace 12 Chevaux," or "replaces twelve horses."

1950s Latil H14 TL 10 Navette

Above: Latil's H14 TL 10 was available with two-way controls so it could be used for either cable-driven or direct plowing. The tractor featured a 45-horsepower, 342-ci (5.6-liter) diesel, eight-speed gearbox, and four-wheel steering and drive. It was available from 1948 into the 1950s. Owner: Pierre Bouillé of Meaux, France.

1950s Latil TL 10

Left: Latil's 50-horsepower four-wheel-drive TL 10 tractor of the 1950s at work with the firm's reversible plow. After pulling the plow to one end of a field, the tractor was simply moved to the other end of the plow for the return trip.

Le Percheron

The name "Le Percheron" came from the breed of heavy draft horses and was an apt moniker for the tractor copied from Heinrich Lanz by the Société Nationale de Construction Aeronautique du Centre. The tractor was powered by a single-cylinder, hot-bulb engine similar to the SFV. Approximately 3,700 were built from the mid-1940s to the end of the enterprise in 1956.

1950s Le Percheron
Above: *Daniel Binet demonstrates the starting procedure for Le Percheron, which is done in the same way as with a Lanz: by using the steering wheel. The 25/27-horsepower hot-bulb engine had a single, 293-ci (4.8-liter) cylinder.*

1950s Le Percheron
Right: *Like the KL Bulldog built in Australia and the Ursus produced in Poland, Le Percheron was a Heinrich Lanz tractor copy. Le Percheron was made until 1957, by which time almost 3,700 had been sold.*

MAP

Made by the Manufacture d'Armes de Paris, the first MAP tractors of 1945 were powered by Latil gas engines. In 1947, MAP replaced the Latil with its own twin-cylinder opposed-four-piston two-stroke diesel with a supercharger.

Using two diesel tractor engines, MAP constructed a racing car in 1949 built on a French Delahaye automobile chassis. The race car broke various diesel records with speeds of up to 120 miles per hour (192 km/h). Unfortunately, the MAP tractor was less successful, although about 15,000 were sold up to the end of production in 1955.

SIMCA (Société Industrielle de Mécanique et de Carrosserie Automobile) acquired MAP in 1952, and MAP's tractors became the basis for SIMCA's first SOMECA (Société de Mécanique de la Seine) tractors in 1953.

RENAULT

By far the most important indigenous French tractor maker is Renault of Billancourt, Paris, which traces its roots back to 1898 and its pioneering work in building automobiles. Renault began tractor experiments in 1908 and was producing various crawlers and four-wheel-drive machines at the time of World War I.

In 1918, Renault transformed its crawlers into farm tractors with their characteristic radiators set at the back of the hood so they were out of harm's way. Wheeled tractors followed in the early 1920s, and diesel experiments began in 1931 culminating in the VY tractor of 1933 with a four-cylinder 266-ci (4.36-liter) engine producing 45 brake horsepower. The VY was the first production diesel tractor in France and was one of the first tractors anywhere with a standardized 875-rpm PTO.

The Renault firm was nationalized in 1945. The new Renault made tractors a priority and turned out 7,500 gas-kerosene types in 1947 and 1948 alone.

From 1951, Renault tractors were powered by Perkins diesel engines made as well as Hercules diesels license-built by Hispano-Suiza. In 1956, Renault unveiled its D series tractors, which culminated in the Super D of 1965 with Tracto Control hydraulics. By 1960, Renault had built a total of 138,000 tractors.

Renault had developed links with the German firm Mannesmann that bought out Porsche's tractor interests, and Mannesmann built tractors for Renault; a

1921 Renault HO
A driver's-eye view from the HO shows that the alligator-style hood gave optimum forward visibility.

further German tie came when Renault tractors began using MWM diesels. After a tractor project in unison with the American Allis-Chalmers firm was aborted, the Renault range was expanded in the early 1970s by the addition of four-wheel-drive Carraro and PGS tractors from Italy, which were sold in France in Renault livery. Renault's Spanish SEMA tractor factory was sold to Spanish tractor maker Ebro in 1975, when power steering, twelve-speed gearboxes, and safety cabs were widely used, and an automatic front differential lock had been perfected for most of the range.

Renault's latest international link has been with John Deere in the mid-1990s, with the two firms mak-

1921 Renault HO

With a history of building crawler tractors, the firm produced one of its first wheeled models with this Renault HO of 1921. The gas tank bears a logo reminding French farmers of the tractor's wartime origins. The HO featured a 22.4-horsepower four-cylinder engine under its alligator-style hood. The sloping radiator set at the back of the engine was designed to be as low as possible and out of harm's way.

ing components for each other and marketing some of the other's tractors through their dealers. Renault also shares a driveline design and manufacturing facility in France with Massey-Ferguson called GIMA. All of these cooperative projects are part of Renault's effort to remain competitive in the French domestic market where Renault is still the leader in tractor production but with only about a sixth of total sales. In 1995, Renault sold about 10,000 tractors.

1930 Renault advertisement
Above: *"The French earth should be farmed by a French tractor,"* implored this patriotic Renault advertisement.

1930 Renault PE2
Left: *The PE2 was produced until 1936. Renault's other tractors of the time included a two-cylinder semi-diesel RKS 10/20 model, a 305-ci (5.0-liter) crawler, and the little YL.*

1930 Renault PE2

The 10/20-horsepower PE2 was powered by a four-cylinder, 129-ci (2.12-liter) gasoline engine and featured three forward gears. Owner: Jean-Claude Cadine of France.

1933 Renault YL

Renault's 8-horsepower YL boasted a 90-ci (1.48-liter) four-cylinder automobile engine. Avid Renault collector Jean-Claude Cadine is at the wheel of his 1933 YL.

1936 Renault RKS

The Renault RKS produced 10/20 horsepower from its two-cylinder, 211-ci (3.45-liter) semi-diesel engine.

1927 Renault PE

Above: *A glimpse under the hood of a 1927 Renault PE reveals the tractor's automobile-derived 14-horsepower engine and vertically mounted radiator.*

1933 Renault YL

Facing page: *The little Renault YL was available for five years starting in 1933.*

1952 Renault P4
A Perkins P4-powered Renault hauls a Merlin threshing machine.

1959 Renault D22
The D22 was powered by a two-cylinder, air-cooled, 110-ci (1.8-liter) engine that fathered 22 horsepower. It had six forward gears with a Borg Warner synchro on the fifth and top speeds.

1951 Renault R 7012
A 22/32-horsepower Renault R 7012 equipped with Rotapede wheels for reduced ground pressure.

SFV and Vierzon

The Société Française de Matériel Agricole et Industriel de Vierzon (known as SFV) stemmed from a farm machinery business founded in 1847 that began building steam engines in 1861.

The first Vierzon gasoline-powered tractor was unveiled in 1931. It was propelled by a single-cylinder, two-stroke, hot-bulb engine producing 50/55 horsepower. Lower-powered models followed, but there were few other changes up to 1957. After World War II, the Vierzon tractors were restyled with more squared-off hoods. At the same time, the Vierzon name was dropped and the initials "SFV" were adopted on the tractors—although French farmers often called them simply "Société." SFV produced 170 tractors and 30 threshing machines per month in 1948, with a peak of almost 5,000 tractors and threshers combined in the whole of 1955.

From the mid-1950s, SFV's business declined until it won a temporary reprieve in the late 1950s when the American Case firm acquired the company. Unfortunately, Case could not stem the downward fall, and despite a tractor restyling with modern fiberglass hoods, the venerable SFV firm went under in the early 1960s. The last SFV tractors were powered by either Peugeot gas engines or full diesel one- and two-cylinder engines from Normag in Germany. Some exclusively French Case tractors were then built for a while at the SFV factory.

1952 SFV 551
The largest SFV in 1952 was the 781-ci (12.8-liter) 551 model with its 52/63 horsepower and five forward gears. The blow lamp is used to aid in starting the hot-bulb engine. The big 551 stands outside a Brittany farmhouse, with the owner's mother, Madame Hingant, and a sheepdog looking on.

1937 SFV H2

Above: *The Société Française Vierzon 25-horsepower H2 tractor was propelled by a hot-bulb single-cylinder engine.*

1937 SFV H2

Left: *Like the Lanz and later Marshalls, the SFV H2 had a sideways-facing radiator and a massive muffler to arrest sparks and some of the noise. This original specimen belongs to Daniel Binet.*

1957 SFV 201

Facing page: *The smallest 1957 SFV was the 195-ci (3.2-liter) 201 model rated at 19 horsepower.*

1954 SFV 201

Above: *A beautifully restored SFV 201 belonging to François Millet is seen at the large Locomotion en Fête agricultural event held each summer at Cerny La Ferté Alais, France.*

1950s SFV 201E advertisement

Left: *The little single-cylinder SFV 201E 25-horse-power tractor was less than 40 inches (1 meter) wide, making it ideal for working vineyards. It was offered from 1953 to 1957.*

1952 SFV 551

Above: *Charles Hingant displays the massive connecting rod and piston of the H2. The cylinder bore and stroke measure a massive 9x10.4 inches (225x260 mm). The H2 is the largest and one of the rarest post–World War II SFV models.*

1960 SFV Super 204

Left: *One of the final SFV models was the 195-ci (3.2-liter) Super 204 with a new hood design and Case color scheme.*

SIFT

Founded by two former Renault tractor employees, the Société d'Installation de Force et de Traction (SIFT) of Boulogne sur Siene started in 1935 but hit the big time 1945 when aero engine giant Gnôme et Rhône became the SNECMA aerospace concern and diversified into civilian products, buying SIFT.

The SIFT was billed as France's first mass-produced diesel tractor. SIFT envisaged building 200 of these 378-ci (6.2-liter) four-cylinder giants per month, but the highest production rate ever achieved was half that, in 1949. The production rate subsequently dwindled rapidly in the coming years due to the success of Ferguson, Massey-Harris, International, SOMECA, and other new arrivals in an already crowded field.

Before SIFT expired in the mid-1960s, the firm's final tractor models included two- and four-cylinder diesel Heracles models.

1950s SIFT
Australian advertisement for the SIFT four-cylinder diesel of 33/42 horsepower.

1957 SIFT TLY
The diesel SIFT of 1957 came with either a two-cylinder 30-horsepower or four-cylinder 45- or 60-horsepower engine. This is the large, 379-ci (6.2-liter) TLY. Owner: Charles Hingant of Brittany, France.

1950s SIMCA SOMECA SOM 40
SOMECA was aligned with SIMCA, which was affiliated with Fiat, thus SOMECA's tractors often used Fiat/OM design and components.

SIMCA AND SOMECA

The Société Industrielle de Mécanique et de Carrosserie Automobile (SIMCA) was founded in 1934 to build Fiat cars under license for the French market. SIMCA also marketed Fiat and Austrian Steyr tractors in France into the 1960s.

SIMCA acquired MAP, and MAP's tractors became the basis for SIMCA's first SOMECA (Société de Mécanique de la Seine) tractors in 1953. SOMECA had begun by supplying components for MAP's later tractors. The first SOMECA was the DA50 developing 37 horsepower at 1500 rpm. Then came the 40 and 55 followed by the similar 615/715. More than 40,000 Fiat-based SOMECA tractors were built by 1960.

Today, Fiat is a majority shareholder in SOMECA and, like the agricultural section of Ford, the firm is part of New Holland.

1960s SOMECA
A mid-1960s SOMECA of obvious Fiat origin. By this time, the SOMECA range spanned models from 67 to 250 ci (1.1 to 4.1 liters) displacement with two- and four-cylinder engines.

VENDEUVRE

The Vendeuvre company of Vendeuvre and Paris began production of farm tractors in 1950 and had sold 25,000 tractors by the time that the American Allis-Chalmers firm bought the business in 1959. Vendeuvre tractors were typically powered by one- and two-cylinder air-cooled engines, although three-cylinder models of up to 244 ci (4 liters) were also available. Tractors were produced in Allis-Chalmers orange up to the closure of the factory in 1964.

1940s Vendeuvre
Above: *Vendeuvre made stationary engines and threshing machines before developing tractors after World War II. This is one of its earliest models, featuring the firm's own four-cylinder diesel.*

1957 Vendeuvre Super
Right: *Vendeuvre made this air-cooled Super model in 1957. The firm ended its days under Allis-Chalmers control in the 1960s.*

Other French Tractor Companies

ADN

Along with St. Chamond and Richard Continental, Aciéries du Nord (ADN), or "Northern Steelworks," was one of the primary French manufacturers of farm crawlers. Starting in the late 1940s, the firm offered an extensive range of tracklayers, including a 132-ci (2.165-liter) twin-cylinder diesel made by Georges Irat, 775-ci (12.7-liter) ADN four, and 1,166-ci (19.1-liter) ADN six.

Agrip

Agrip of Ligniéres started around 1950 by converting war-surplus American Jeep chassis for farm use, soon fitting them with Aster diesels and larger rear wheels. By the 1970s, Agrip offered powerful, purpose-built four-wheel-drive tractors, although most were employed for industrial rather than agricultural purposes.

Babiole, Derot-Tecnoma, and Sabatier

The only others to make any serious inroads in the past fifty years have been Babiole, Derot-Tecnoma (vineyard models), and Sabatier, while in the early years there were dozens of firms with good ideas but few farmers wealthy enough to support them.

Ceres

Ceres built a few tractors of its own in the 1920s. The firm later went into the business of converting other tractors, such as the popular Massey-Harris Pony, to run on diesel.

Champion

Champion offered an extensive range of wheeled tractors in the 1950s with diesel engines from Ceres. Champion was briefly successful, selling over 1,000 tractors annually in the mid-1950s.

ECO

The ECO tractor first appeared in 1938 powered by a two-cylinder Mercedes-Benz diesel engine. The ECO lasted well into the 1950s, fitted with Poyaud and Aster diesels. As with so many other hopeful makers, sales were small; In ECO's case, total sales probably amounted to only about 1,000 tractors total over all of its years of production.

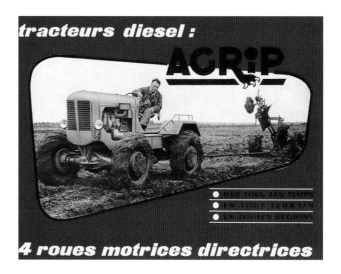

1950s Agrip
Agrip grew from converting military-surplus vehicles for agricultural use to building this sophisticated four-wheel-drive tractor in the 1950s. Power came from either a 20-horsepower Aster diesel or 30-horsepower CLM diesel.

Energic

Établissements Patissier's Energic from Villefranche, Rhône, started life as an artisan-assembled light tractor, becoming more sophisticated through the 1950s. The Energic was powered by Citroën automobile engines.

Mecavia

Mecavia of Autun was associated with both MAP and SOMECA in the mid-1950s.

Richard Continental

Richard Continental of Lyons, also known as simply Continental, made crawler machines primarily for the construction industry, similar to the American Caterpillar. In the 1940s and 1950s, Continental offered tracked agricultural tractors with ratings ranging from 17 to 70 horsepower.

St. Chamond

The St. Chamond company of St. Chamond, Loire, built military crawlers at the time of World War I, but did not become widely known for agricultural tractors until the 1950s. The St. Chamond farm tractors were small crawlers often powered by Perkins diesel engines of 134 to 330 ci (2.2 to 5.4 liters).

1948 Richard Continental catalog

Right, top: *By 1948, Richard Continental was offering crawlers with ratings from 32 to 58 drawbar horsepower. Berliet, Irat, and Panhard engines were used.*

1950s Energic 511

Right, bottom: *Typical of the basic tractors available from Energic in the early 1950s was the 43-ci (700-cc) single-cylinder 511 model.*

1948 ECO

Below: *This 1948 ECO featured a 50-horsepower Poyaud two-cylinder marine-type diesel engine. Few ECOs survive from a brief production run that ended in the mid-1950s. Owner: Charles Hingant of Brittany, France.*

GERMANY

Like the other heavily industrialized countries, Germany, with its dependence on farming to feed a growing population, was quick to mechanize farming. Many of the German agricultural equipment makers' early efforts were directed towards motor plows, some of which resembled two-wheeled garden cultivator tractors scaled up to massive proportions. Motor plow development continued into the 1920s, but then hit a dead end.

German manufacturers realized in the 1920s that the way of the future was with more compact machines that were able to accomplish other duties than simply plowing and belt work. Some of these machines were effectively compact versions of World War I gun tractors, which had reached a relatively sophisticated stage with winches and, in some cases, four-wheel drive.

1939 Lanz HR9 Eil Bulldog
Facing page: *The Lanz HR9 "Speedy" Bulldog belonging to well-known French Lanz collector Pierre Bouillé prepares to set out on the road.*

1954 Hanomag catalog
Above: *A 1954 Swedish catalog for Hanomag pictures the various types of R35 crawlers and wheeled tractors available.*

The pioneering diesel tractor of Benz in the early 1920s signaled a revolution in German farm tractors and truly marked the end for the draft horse. In the 1930s, ahead of virtually all other countries, several German firms adopted full diesel power; at the end of the decade, a spate of newcomers to the tractor market such as Eicher and Schlüter made their names with diesels.

Many other German tractor makers relied on a different style of engine: the hot-bulb engine that ran on heavy oil. Hot-bulb engines were favored by Heinrich Lanz with its famous one-cylinder design of 1921 and used for years after.

German makers also gave birth to several types of tractors that are unique. One unusual German development was the multi-purpose four-wheel-drive Unimog, which eventually spawned the MB-Trac from Mercedes-Benz. Another type of machine seldom seen elsewhere was the rear-engined multi-purpose load-carrying tractor exemplified by the Fendt F 275GT, Eicher Kombi, and Lanz Alldog. As in other wine-growing regions, several firms have made ultra-narrow vineyard models, often with four-wheel drive and equal-sized wheels.

As in Great Britain, there were many hopeful entrants into the lightweight tractor sector around 1950, but few of these firms made the grade in the difficult economic conditions of the post–World War II years. Even old, established businesses were swallowed up by American multinationals, such as Deere & Company's acquisition of Heinrich Lanz in 1955. The surviving firms had competition on their own soil from giants like International Harvester, which established its own factories in Germany after World War II. Still, between 1945 and 1960, the German tractor industry sold 69,000 machines into neighboring France, which was well ahead of the totals of the other great exporters, the United States and Britain.

As in other parts of the world, there has been a great reduction in the number of individual tractor firms in recent years, but Germany still remains a major force in the global tractor business. Recent consolidations have seen Deutz join SAME and AGCO acquire Fendt in 1997.

1923 MWM Motorpferd
Through the years, Motoren-Werke Mannheim (MWM) made engines for many tractor manufacturers, but the firm started as an offshoot of Benz and made this Motorpferd, or "Motorhorse," in 1923. It had a 269-ci (4.4-liter) two-cylinder semi-diesel engine that fathered 16/18 horsepower. Owner: Frans Nouwen of Heythuysen, the Netherlands.

DAIMLER, BENZ, AND MERCEDES-BENZ

Daimler, whose cars became known as Mercedes, and Benz were two pioneering motor firms whose first vehicles took to the road in 1885–1886. The two firms merged to form Daimler-Benz, the forerunner of today's Mercedes-Benz, in 1925–1926, by which time both had made tractors.

Daimler was first, crafting a gasoline-powered tractor in 1912, but the more significant tractor was the diesel-engined Benz of 1922. The Benz diesel was developed to best all other tractors in the German market of the late 1920s, but went out of production in the Great Depression of the 1930s. Still, the Benz goes down in history as the first production diesel tractor, setting the stage for diesel development over the next decades.

Daimler-Benz returned to the agricultural market with the multi-purpose four-wheel-drive Unimog in 1950; the Unimog had been independently produced by Boehringer Brothers for several years. Load-carrying Unimogs fitted with PTOs and three-point hitches were widely used in farming until the more specialized MB-Trac appeared in 1973. Ten thousand MB-Tracs were made by 1980, but Mercedes-Benz sold the design during the subsequent economic recession to a consortium that by then also controlled Schlüter.

1922 Benz tractor brochure
In the early 1920s, Benz's pioneering diesel tractor spelled doom for the draft horse.

1930s Mercedes-Benz tractor advertisement
Above, top: *The Mercedes-Benz two-cylinder 30-horsepower diesel tractor was sold by steam engineers J. & H. McLaren as the McLaren Diesel Oil Tractor through the Midland Engine Works of Leeds, Great Britain, during the early 1930s.*

1950 Nordtrak Diesel Stier
Above, bottom: *Nordtrak's Stier, or "Bull," used a Hatz 13-horsepower single-cylinder diesel with axles from ex–U.S. Army four-wheel-drive vehicles. Owner: Nijsen Corry of Bocholt, Belgium.*

Deutz and Fahr

Deutz pioneered the use of Nikolas Otto's revolutionary four-cycle internal-combustion engine and first made farm tractors with the novel engine in 1907. During World War I, the firm built heavy military tractors used principally for gun towing.

In 1926, Deutz built its first lightweight tractor, the 14-horsepower MTH 222, joined a year later by a diesel version. After steady development through the 1930s, Deutz began to make air-cooled diesel engines in 1942, which were applied to tractors from 1949. In 1954, Deutz added a clever long, nearly horizontal steering column to allow seating on either side of the tractor for different directions of operation. By 1954, 50,000 Deutz tractors had been sold.

In 1968–1969, Deutz merged with Fahr. Fahr had made tractors since 1938, often powered by Deutz engines in the early years but later featuring Guldner units. The combined firm became Deutz-Fahr, and its tractor production spread to Yugoslavia and Argentina.

Starting in 1972, the forward-control Intrac was developed into a multi-purpose farming system. In 1995, the tractor and implement business was acquired by SAME of Italy, whilst the Deutz tractor interests in Argentina went to AGCO in 1997.

1907 Deutz Pfuglokomotive
Below, top: *Detuz's 1907 Pfuglokomotive, or "Plow-locomotive," weighed a massive 3 tons (2,700 kg). It was powered by a 25-horsepower engine geared to a maximum of 3 miles per hour (5 km/h) forwards and backwards.*

1919 Deutz
Below, bottom: *This massive 40-horsepower Deutz winch tractor was built in 1919, but owed its origin to World War I gun tractors.*

1932–1934 Deutz MTZ 320
Facing page: *Deutz's MTZ 320 had a two-cylinder 391-ci (6.4-liter) diesel and three forward gears, providing a maximum speed of 4 miles per hour (6.3 km/h).*

1950s Deutz FL
Above: *Photographed in southern Bavaria, this mid-1950s Deutz was part of the FL range that was available in one-, two-, and three-cylinder versions.*

1954 Deutz
Left: *This lightweight Deutz tractor was powered by a 45-ci (736-cc) single-cylinder, air-cooled diesel. The driver could turn around and sit in front of the steering wheel to operate the tractor in the opposite direction.*

1964 Deutz D80
Above, top: *The D80 was Deutz's powerhouse. It was propelled by a six-cylinder 75-horsepower air-cooled diesel and boasted power steering as a standard feature. Owner: Jan Nijssen of Helden, the Netherlands.*

1963 Deutz D 25S
Above, bottom: *The Deutz D 25S featured a two-cylinder, air-cooled 104-ci (1.7-liter) diesel. Owner: Jan Nijssen of Helden, the Netherlands.*

1960 Fahr D177S brochure
The 34-horsepower Fahr D177S featured a hydraulic implement lift.

EICHER

The Eicher brothers began to make Deutz-engined tractors in 1936, building their 1,000th tractor in 1941. Eicher developed its own air-cooled diesel in 1948, featuring two-, three-, and four-cylinder versions. The Wotan model of 1968 boasted a large six-cylinder diesel.

For a time in the 1970s, Massey-Ferguson of Canada owned a stake in the business, and water-cooled Perkins-engined models were added to the range as Massey then owned Perkins.

In the mid-1980s, the 120,000th Eicher tractor was built, and the company was making about 2,000 tractors annually. By that time, the firm had become a smaller, more specialized enterprise making predominantly four-wheel-drive tractors with sixteen forward Synchron gears.

1958 Eicher brochure
Right: *The air-cooled, 159-ci (2.6-liter), two-cylinder Eicher of 1958 had 26 horsepower available.*

1954 Eicher EKL11
Below: *This EKL11, with its single-cylinder, 92-ci (1.5-liter) Deutz diesel engine, was still in regular use in the 1990s. Note the leaf springs in lieu of a conventional front axle.*

FENDT

Commencing in 1928 with self-propelled mowers, Fendt of Marktoberdorf soon developed its multipurpose Dieselross tractors with Deutz diesels. MWM diesels predominated after the war with either air or water cooling. The Dieselross was a small tractor, but Fendt began building larger models using its own engines in the Farmer and Favorit of the 1960s. Fendt was early into the rear-engined tool-frame type of machine in the 1950s with its GT models. In the 1970s, it also made complete four-wheel-drive Agrobil forage cutters and loaders.

After MAN left the tractor business, Fendt began to use MAN engines in its largest tractors. The most powerful MAN-powered model in the mid-1990s was the Xylon with 260 brake horsepower.

By the 1990s, more than 600,000 Fendts had been sold, including some models from a Brazilian factory in the 1960s, and the firm was building some 15,000 of its high-quality machines each year. In 1997, Fendt was acquired by AGCO of the United States.

1938 Fendt Dieselross F 22
Above, top: *Fendt's Dieselross, or "Diesel-horse," began as a "stationery engine on wheels." By the time the F 22 was made in 1938, the tractor had become a much more orthodox machine.*

1954 Fendt Dieselross F 20
Above, bottom: *The F 20 featured a single-cylinder MWM diesel.*

1963 Fendt Farmer 2 brochure
The three-cylinder, 122-ci (2.0-liter) Fendt Farmer 2 of 1963 had eight forward and four reverse gears.

HANOMAG

Hanomag is a shortened version of Hannoversche Maschinenbau AG (Hannover Machine Works), and the firm originally made steam locomotives and other types of machinery. It entered the vehicle business in 1905 and built its WD motor plows from 1912. Crawler and wheeled tractors joined the line in 1919. From 1930, most models were diesel powered using a 317-ci (5.2-liter) four-cylinder that was produced for the next thirty-five years. In 1942, five-speed gearboxes were standardized, and from the mid-1950s, the smallest one- and two-cylinder engines were two-strokes. Hanomag's range then covered tractors from 16 to 90 horsepower, the largest being a crawler.

In 1957, the firm became a pioneer of turbocharging, having previously offered supercharging on the 1953 R12 combined tool-frame tractor and load carrier that became well known as the Combitrac.

In 1961, Hanomag's new masters in the Rheinstal group bought the Borgward car and truck factory and gained a new 109-ci (1.8-liter) diesel for the tractors. Larger models were still supercharged, but the days of old, hard-working diesels were numbered, and an advanced, new range was launched in 1967. Unfortunately it did not sell well, and after producing a grand total of 250,000 tractors, Hanomag ceased production in 1971. The Hanomag-Henschel truck business was then sold to Daimler-Benz, while the crawler loaders were adopted by Massey-Ferguson in 1974. Following various changes in ownership, Japan's Kubota gained control of Hanomag in 1989.

1960 Hanomag R 455 ATK
The R 455 ATK was an industrial version of the R 450 agricultural tractor. This Hanomag started its life towing aircraft in Germany. Owner: W. V. D. Putten of the Netherlands.

1947–1948 Hanomag R 40
Facing page, top: *Looking rakish with its road equipment, this Hanomag R 40 was originally used for hauling vegetables to market in Germany. The R 40 was developed in the late 1930s and had a four-cylinder 317-ci (5.2-liter) diesel rated at 40 horsepower. Owner: Hank van Doorn of the Netherlands.*

1950s Hanomag R 228
Facing page, bottom: *This export model R 228 Hanomag was unusual in the mid- to late-1950s range for being a two stroke, and it soon earned a reputation for unreliability. Owner: Hank van Doorn of the Netherlands.*

1930s Hanomag brochure
In this late 1930s French brochure, Hanomag claimed to have had the first diesel tractor factory in Europe, although others like Benz would surely have had rival claims.

Heinrich Lanz

Heinrich Lanz of Mannheim crafted steam traction engines before building massive motor cultivators in 1912.

In 1921, Lanz created a self-propelled stationary engine with a hot-bulb multi-fuel two-stroke engine that became a great success. Soon known as the Bulldog, the Lanz was available with engines of between 380 and 862 ci (6.23 and 14.13 liters) in the early years. An amusing feature of the Bulldog was the detachable steering wheel plugged into the side-mounted flywheel for starting purposes once a blow lamp had heated the cylinder head.

The famous Bulldog lasted until 1956, by which time about 200,000 had been sold. After Lanz acquired the Hungarian HSCS in 1938, Bulldogs were also made in HSCS's Vienna, Austria, factory. Bulldogs were made in Madrid, Spain, from 1946 to 1962; Bulldog copies also appeared in Poland, France, and Australia.

In 1955, Lanz was acquired by the American Deere & Company. Under Deere's control, the Lanz works built multi-cylinder, vertical-engined tractors, initially under the name John Deere Lanz; some models featured Perkins diesels. By the 1970s, the venerable German name disappeared, although its famous factory at Mannheim made the bulk of John Deere tractors for the European market, even exporting tractors back to the United States.

Hermann Lanz and Hela

Another tractor bearing the Lanz name was built by Hermann Lanz of Aulendorf and first appeared in 1929. Lanz renamed its machines Hela after World War II to avoid the inevitable confusion with the Heinrich Lanz tractors.

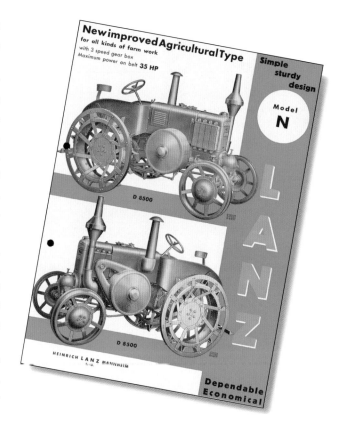

1930s Lanz Bulldog D 8500 brochure
Above: *Classic single-cylinder, hot-bulb-engined Lanz D 8500 Model N Bulldogs on lug wheels with road bands. This model featured 35 horsepower on tap. This brochure came from the British importer, Lanz Tractor Company, Ltd., of London.*

1920s Lanz HR4 prototype
Below: *This prototype HR4 Lanz rode on solid-rubber-tired wheels and retractable spikes. The HR series entered production in 1928 and was revised for 1935.*

1939 Lanz Eil Bulldog HR9
Facing page, top: *Leo "Lanz" Speer outside his Landmaschinen museum in Rimbach, Germany.*

1939 Lanz Eil Bulldog HR9
Facing page, bottom: *The Eil Bulldog boasted a comfortable driving environment protected by a full windshield. Note the long transverse fuel tank behind the bench seat.*

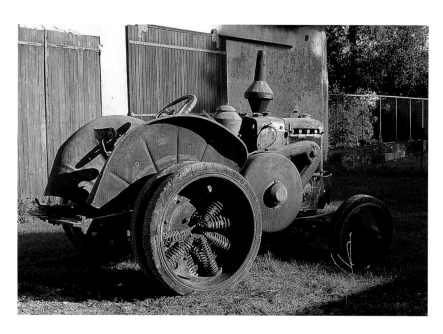

1952 Lanz Bulldog D 2206

Left: *The little Lanz 22-horsepower model of 1952 had a single-cylinder engine of 138-ci (2.26-liter) displacement that was able to run on a wide range of crude fuels. In the highest of its six gears, 12½ miles per hour (20 km/h) was claimed; in the lowest gear, it could tow a 20-ton (18,000-kg) load.*

1939 Lanz Eil Bulldog HR9

Above: *The front of the road-equipped Eil Bulldog HR9 of 1939. The model was available from 1937, when 185 were built; 1939 marked the peak production year with 528 built.*

1939 Lanz Eil Bulldog HR9

Left: *This Eil, or "Speedy," Bulldog was built in 1939 and powered by a large 629-ci (10.3-liter) engine. These Bulldog road models had five or six forward gears that could be changed on the move and a top speed of 25 miles per hour (40 km/h).*

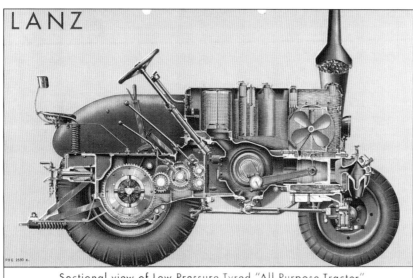

Sectional view of Low Pressure Tyred "All Purpose Tractor"
with six speeds forward and electric equipment

1951 Lanz Bulldog D 9506
Above, top: *The D 9506 Bulldog had a 45-horsepower hot-bulb engine of a massive 629-ci (10.3-liter) displacement. Owner: Daniel Binet of Normandy, France.*

1950s Lanz Bulldog sectional drawing
Above, bottom: *Powerline details of a typical single-cylinder Lanz Bulldog with sprung front axle.*

1950 Lanz Bulldog D 7506
The Bulldog models fitted with pneumatic tires were called Ackerluft, *literally "field air." The D 7506 Bulldog was rated at 25 horsepower. Owner: Jim Thomas of Wokingham, Great Britain.*

1954 Lanz B Bulldog D 2806

Above: *The D 2806 of 1954 had a 28-horsepower, 226-ci (3.7-liter), single-cylinder engine.*

1950s Lanz Bulldog Model T brochure

Right: *Lanz also offered crawler versions of its famous Bulldog, including the 55-horsepower Model T available in this Australian brochure.*

1954 Lanz B Bulldog D 2806

Facing page: *Owner Daniel Binet with his son, Yoann, on the Lanz Bulldog D 2806. Many contemporary German tractors had fender seats.*

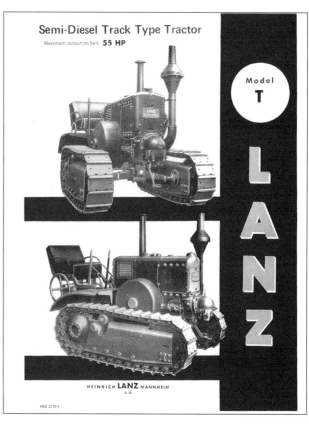

Semi-Diesel Track Type Tractor
Maximum output on belt **55 HP**

Model
T

LANZ

HEINRICH **LANZ** MANNHEIM
A.-G.

MAN

Maschinenfabrik Augsburg-Nürnberg (MAN) collaborated with Dr. Rudolf Diesel in developing the first diesel engines, in 1897. MAN made trucks from 1915; from 1924, the trucks were powered by four-cylinder diesels.

Following limited success with motor plows, MAN introduced in 1924 a line of farm tractors using four-cylinder diesel engines similar to that of its trucks.. Demand again proved to be small, and the tractors were abandoned after a few years.

In 1938, MAN entered the tractor field again, offering the 50-horsepower AS 250, which was available until World War II production intervened. MAN took control of the French Latil factory's output during the war to built materiel.

MAN's next foray into the agricultural market came in 1949 with 25-horsepower models that were remarkable for being built with either two- or four-wheel drive. All-wheel drive soon became a MAN forte on all of its tractors from 25 to 45 horsepower. However, its commercial vehicles became far bigger business, and in 1958, the tractor side was linked with Porsche tractors. In 1962, the new owners of Porsche tractors, Mannesmann, built the last of some 40,000 MAN tractors to have been sold since the firm's first tractor of 1924.

1959 MAN 4S2

Right: *Christian Denis looks out from the cab of his 1959 4S2 that is equipped with all the factory options. On the grille, the initials of Maschinenfabrik Augsburg-Nürnberg surmount the script "Ackerdiesel," or "field diesel," and historic badges.*

1955 MAN AS440H

Facing page, top: *The AS440H was one of MAN's unusual two-wheel-drive models. It was powered by a four-cylinder, 40-horsepower diesel.*

1959 MAN 4S2

Facing page, bottom: *The four-wheel-drive 4S2 was normally powered by a 50-horsepower, four-cylinder diesel, but this tractor has a powerhouse six-cylinder, 120-horsepower MAN diesel. Owner: Christian Denis of Limbourg, Belgium.*

1961 MAN 4N2 brochure
Above: *The 4N2 featured a two-cylinder, 28-horsepower, water-cooled diesel and four-wheel drive.*

1961 MAN 4R3
Right: *The 4R3 MAN of 1961 was powered by a 45-horsepower, four-cylinder diesel. The tractor had four-wheel drive and a rear-mounted winch for forestry work. Owner: Christian Denis of Limbourg, Belgium.*

1961 MAN 2KZ
A 1961 21-horsepower MAN 2KZ with extended wheelbase for mid-mounted finger mower. The grille-mounted "M" badge signified a patented low-noise swirl combustion system developed in 1954.

PORSCHE AND ALLGAIER

Dr. Ferdinand Porsche is famous for his Volkswagen and Porsche cars, but he also designed and built several tractor models over the years. During World War I, Porsche worked for Austro-Daimler of Austro-Hungary, where he developed large four-wheel-drive gun tractors as well as a lightweight farm tractor prototype.

Working in Germany in 1937, Porsche revived his Austro-Daimler tractor prototype to create his *Volksschlepper*, or "People's Tractor," in much the same way that his Volkswagen was to be a People's Car. The tractor featured a gasoline-fueled air-cooled engine mounted in the rear; load space was in the front. A small number of Porsche's *Volksschleppers* were built from 1938 into the early years of World War II.

In 1945, the People's Tractor idea was revived by a forerunner of Porsche's sports car firm, but this time the tractor featured a front-mounted, twin-cylinder air-cooled diesel.

Allgaier made some primitive hopper-cooled single-cylinder tractors from 1946, but in 1949, the company adopted the Porsche tractor and built about 25,000 Allgaier Porsches until 1957, when the firm reverted to its machine-tool specialty.

At this stage, the Mannesmann group acquired the Porsche tractor license and moved production from Uhingen to Friedrichshafen. The German Mannesmann engineering conglomerate took over MAN's tractor interests in 1958 and built Porsche tractors; the range then included one-, two-, three-, and four-cylinder Junior, Standard, Super, and Master models spanning 14 to 50 horsepower with 90 percent parts commonality. In 1964, Renault of France took over Mannesmann's tractor interests, and the Porsche name disappeared from the tractor field.

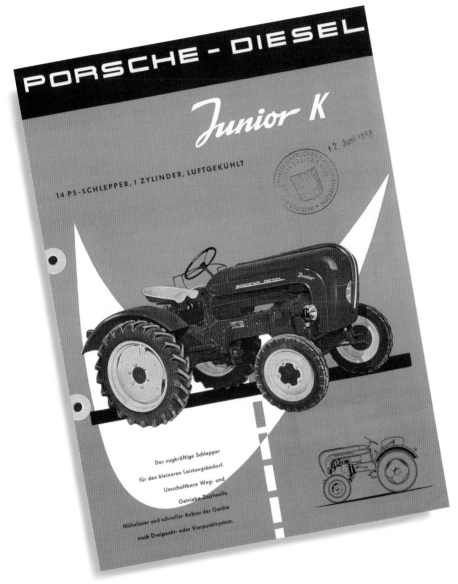

1958 Porsche Junior K brochure
Left: *A 1958 brochure for the Junior K air-cooled, single-cylinder, 14-horse-power Porsche. The tractor boasted six forward and two reverse gears, a 540/2000-rpm PTO, and hydraulic lift.*

1959 Porsche Junior V
Below, left: *An original 1959 Porsche Junior V still in use. The small Porsche was powered by a single-cylinder, air-cooled, 49-ci (0.8-liter) diesel. Owner: Herr Grossman of Taufkirchen, Bavaria, Germany.*

1950 Allgaier
Below, right: *This 1950 Allgaier was considered a "stationary engine on wheels." Power came from the Kaelble hopper-cooled, single-cylinder, 18-horsepower engine. Owners: Andrew and Chris Hecks.*

SCHLÜTER

Three generations—grandfather, father, and son, all by the name of Anton Schlüter—have run the Schlüter firm since its establishment in 1899. Engines for industrial and farming use were the company's early specialty.

In 1937, Schlüter created its first tractor, powered by a horizontal single-cylinder diesel. Most subsequent models had one- or two-cylinder vertical diesels. During the first twenty years, the firm was prolific, building some 30,000 tractors.

In the 1960s, Schlüter was amongst the first in Europe to move dramatically up the power range. It offered some impressive models, often with four-wheel drive: Four-, six-, and even seven-cylinder types were available with ratings up to 135 horsepower. Luxury cabs were optional from 1966. In 1969, Schlüter launched a turbocharged 580-ci (9.5-liter) straight eight developing 180 horsepower. In the 1970s, MAN engines were used in some models, culminating in the 500-horsepower V-12 Super-Trac of 1978.

Around 1980, Schlüter debuted tractors with hydraulically tilted cabs and four-wheel steering with equal-sized wheels all around. These new models had Schlüter's own six- or eight-cylinder engines with ratings up to 200 horsepower (the sixes were also supplied to Hanomag's crawlers) or MAN sixes of up to 748 ci (12.25 liters).

The market for these expensive, specialized machines was small. Schlüter nearly went out of business when one of the best markets, Yugoslavia (which had bought 600 tractors by 1982), was lost due to financial difficulties and the subsequent civil war. Schlüter had several changes of ownership in recent decades, and now belongs to Schleppertile Egelseer GmbH, which has also acquired the rights to the Mercedes-Benz MB-Trac.

1940s Schlüter brochure
Faced with World War II oil shortages, many German tractor makers built machines to run on producer gas, a gas substitute for gasoline made from adding water to heated anthracite, coal, wood, or other combustibles. This 25/28-horsepower Schlüter could tow 15 tons (13,500 kg).

1939 Schlüter DZM25
This 1939 Schlüter is one of the oldest surviving tractors from the venerable maker. It features a 165-ci (2.7-liter) two-cylinder, 25-horsepower diesel with four forward gears. It was given to owner Nick Baldwin by Bavarian farmer Fritz Nischwitz of Freising in the early 1980s.

1953 Schlüter AS 15D
Above: *This 1953 15-horsepower Schlüter has electric starting and a lever to change the shape of the pre-combustion
chamber for easier detonation. Power comes from the 98-ci
(1.6-liter), single-cylinder engine with five forward gears.
Owner: Nick Baldwin of Barrington, Somerset, Great Britain.*

1955 Schlüter AS 15 brochure
Left: *This 1955 Schlüter AS 15 featured a 92-ci (1.5-liter),
15-horsepower, water-cooled engine and five forward and one
reverse gears.*

OTHER GERMAN TRACTOR COMPANIES

Bautz

Bautz made harvest machinery before introducing MWM-engined tractors in 1948. The firm later built larger-horsepower British Nuffield tractors under license. These lasted through to the early 1960s when Bautz linked up with Hanomag.

Bungartz

Bungartz made tractors in the 1930s but became best known for narrow-track vineyard machines in the 1950s and 1960s, often powered by Hatz air-cooled engines.

Guldner

Guldner provided engines to other tractor makers, such as Fahr, but was also a relatively important tractor maker in its own right from 1936 until well into the 1960s.

FAMO

FAMO made a specialty of building crawlers from the mid-1930s to the late 1950s. The firm also offered some wheeled tractor models.

Hatz

Hatz provided engines to other tractor makers, such as the Bungartz vineyard machines. Hartz also offered a range of tractors from 1953 to 1964 with ratings from 10 to 35 horsepower.

1959 Hatz TL 33

Above: *Like MWM, Hatz made engines for other firms, but also built complete tractors starting in 1954. This is the only known surviving Hatz TL 33. Owner: Corry Nijsen of Bocholt, Belgium.*

1961 Bungartz T5 and 1968 T5E

Starting in the 1930s, Bungartz specialized in compact vineyard tractors for forty years. On the left is a 1961 16-horsepower T5; on the right, a 1968 13-horsepower T5E. Both tractors featured Hatz air-cooled diesels. The drivers are Bart and Johan Sauwen of Belgium.

1950s Hatz T 13
Above: *This T 13 is one of the earliest models of Hatz tractors. It was powered by a 68-ci (1.12-liter), single-cylinder, water-cooled diesel. Owner: Corry Nijsen of Bocholt, Belgium.*

1955 Normag Kornett 1
Below: *Starting in the mid-1930s, Normag was another of the smaller makers in Germany and continued to build tractors for some twenty years. The Kornett 1 had a single-cylinder, 79-ci (1.3-liter), 12/14-horsepower, two-stroke diesel with scavenge pump. This was one of Normag's later models.*

Kramer
Kramer of Gutmadingen built tractors in the 1950s, culminating in Unimog-type machines. The firm still exists in the mechanical handling field.

Normag
Normag made tractors from 1938 and used O+K engines in its final 1956 40-horsepower tractor models. The firm ended its days involved with the Mannesmann conglomerate that acquired the Porsche tractor business.

O+K
Founded by Benno Orenstein and Arthur Koppel in Berlin in 1876, the O+K crane firm offered tractors at several stages from the 1930s through the 1950s.

Stihl
Stihl, famous today for its chainsaws, offered tractors from 1948 to 1960.

GREAT BRITAIN

Tractor makers in Great Britain have long been pioneers and innovators. Steam pioneers include Clayton, McLaren, Fowler, Foden, Marshall, Garrett, and Aveling-Porter. Then there were newcomers to the tractor field from other backgrounds, including Nuffield, Leyland, Turner, Austin, and Bristol. In addition, firms like Petter, Ransomes, Sharp, Ivel, and Saunderson were among the first in the world to craft relatively lightweight and practical agrimotors, as tractors were originally called in Britain.

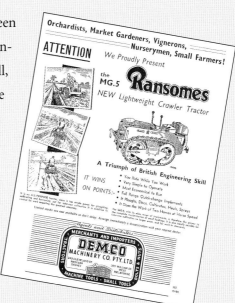

Every motor manufacturing nation commenced with dozens of early tractor hopefuls, few of which made the grade. But in Britain, inventors came up with interesting ideas, such as the 1910 Ideal with its "modern" engine-under-front-hood layout, PTO, and powered implement lift. In addition, the four-wheel-drive Darby-Maskell of 1913 boasted a mechanically operated rotary cultivator. There were hundreds of other makers—some good, some bad. Others were innovative but failed to survive, such as Sentinel, Foden, and Mann, who all tried to popularize lightweight steam tractors rather than heavy agricultural engines. Perhaps not surprisingly, they had all failed by the mid-1930s.

1955 Marshall IIIA
Facing page: *This Marshall IIIA had a 299-ci (4.9-liter), single-cylinder, two-stroke diesel. Owner: Malcolm Goddard of Tiverton, Great Britain.*

Above: **1950s Ransomes MG5 advertisement**

Thanks in large part to its long association with North American tractor makers, Britain became the world's largest tractor exporter following World War II. In 1948, British tractor production exceeded 100,000 units annually for the first time, and topped 200,000 in 1962, of which some 75 percent was typically exported. Ford of England became the largest manufacturer following the move of Fordson Standard production to Dagenham in the 1930s. American firms International and Allis-Chalmers established major factories in Britain before World War II, exporting tractors worldwide and contributing to England's export strength; Case later bought International's factory, where some of today's Case Internationals are manufactured. Canada's Massey-Harris also set up a British factory after World War II, and when Massey acquired Ferguson in 1953, another international giant was born.

1930s Garrett Traction Roadless advertisement
Right, top: *Garrett made the frame for the AGE tractor as well as this Traction Roadless crawler, which continued in production with a Gardner 33/38-horsepower diesel after the collapse of the AGE group.*

1950s International BWD-6
Right, center: *The British-built International BWD-6 was available from 1954 to 1958. It was a large, 50.5-horsepower machine with a big four-cylinder diesel.*

1960 Allis-Chalmers ED-40
Right, bottom: *This Allis-Chalmers ED-40 was built in 1960 in Essendine, Lincolnshire, not far from the home of Marshall. It had a Standard-built four-cylinder, 40-horsepower Ricardo-influenced diesel. The Essendine factory closed in 1968.*

ECONOMICAL POWER

Austin

45-55 H.P. DIESEL TRACTOR.

Modern farming requires the use of newer forms of power.

By greatly reducing the running costs, increasing the output, and the ability of being able to take advantage of all favourable weather conditions, the 45-55 H.P. AUSTIN DIESEL TRACTOR, represents an enormous superiority over older and obsolete forms of farm power

The 45-55 H.P. AUSTIN DIESEL TRACTOR, fitted with low pressure pneumatic tyres, can work on the land or travel on the highways without the extra work of changing over wheel equipment. Used in conjunction with a threshing outfit, or an agricultural trailer, it makes an ideal combination. For ploughing or other land work, the tyre treads dig in and give all the necessary grip on almost every type of soil.

Other wheel equipment consists of steel front and rear wheels, with quick detachable rear wheel rims fitted with efficient cleats, giving maximum adherence under worst conditions.

For further information, please address your inquiries to:—

1930s Austin Diesel brochure

Above: *The British Austin tractor developed along independent lines in France in the 1920s and 1930s, and culminated in this 446-ci (7.3-liter) diesel six-plow model with 45/55 horsepower.*

1930s Austin Diesel

Below: *The French Austin factory at Liancourt was run by Robert Rothschild, who also imported Hanomags into France. This is an early 1930s diesel model with geared-down starting handle.*

AUSTIN

There were many similarities between Henry Ford and Herbert Austin. Both came from farming backgrounds, and both realized the potential of mass production. Austin, who was born in 1866 and was thus three years younger than Ford, found ways of revolutionizing mechanical sheep shears at Wolseley before making a fortune from building his eponymous cars.

During World War I, Great Britain's farm workers and horses were mobilized for the war effort, and so the country was in dire need of tractors to avert famine; Herbert Austin represented the British Government in a search for suitable American tractors. The logical choice was Henry Ford's Fordson, and the selection of the revolutionary lightweight tractor became an important event for both Ford and Austin.

Herbert Austin liked American vehicles and based his post–World War I Austin Twenty car on his favorite Hudson. As with Ford's 20-horsepower automobile, Austin sought economies of scale by using the same 20-horsepower Austin engine in tractors, trucks, and cars. His 1919 tractor bore more than a passing resemblance to the Fordson and was made at a peak rate of sixty-six per week. However, Austin's tractor plans soon went wrong when the imported Fordson undercut his tractors, and a tax on car horsepower decimated the sales of large-engined cars in Britain.

Austin bought a farm and factory in tariff-protected France at Liancourt, and here his tractors were made. Austin even exported his French-built tractors to Britain, although limited British production continued until 1927.

At the 1933 Paris Agricultural Show, Austin displayed a new range of larger, gas-kerosene tractors with up to 55 horsepower. A 45/55-horsepower diesel model followed, built in France long before Austin made a diesel vehicle in Britain.

Austin's tractor venture came to an end with the arrival of World War II. Austin Director Robert Rothschild and some of his colleagues were killed by the Nazis, and German armaments giant Krupp took over Austin's French factory.

BLACKSTONE AND GARRETT

Blackstone was an implement maker that introduced lamp-start oil engines in 1896. In 1912, the firm developed a remarkable diesel-type engine that employed a blower to vaporize a fuel oil similar to kerosene and fired it with spark ignition. Thus, the engine could be started from cold and did not require either the heating of a hot bulb or gasoline to run the engine until it was hot enough to switch to kerosene. A three-cylinder 25-horsepower version of this engine was mounted in a "creeper-track," or crawler, tractor at the end of World War I and, along with wheeled versions, was produced until 1925.

In 1929, Blackstone built diesel engines for fellow members of the short-lived Agricultural & General Engineers (AGE) group. Garrett of Leiston, Suffolk, assembled a small number of these tractors, which were badged as both AGE and Garrett models. They were the world's first high-speed multi-cylinder diesel tractors, whose other design features owed much to the International 15/30. In the 1930 World Tractor Trials, the 36-horsepower machine plowed for more than 1,500 hours with only one stop.

When AGE collapsed in the early 1930s, Blackstone continued as an engine builder, becoming part of the Lister group in 1937.

BRISTOL

Bristol crafted an ingenious light crawler with rubber tracks and a 73-ci (1.2-liter) Douglas air-cooled flat-twin engine that was launched in the early 1930s by Walter Hill, who had worked for Fordson.

In the mid-1930s, William Jowett of Jowett Cars took control of the business. Jowett had been supplying water-cooled versions of the Douglas engines to the Bristol tractors. From 1938 to 1942, diesel versions with Coventry-Victor horizontal twins were also offered.

After World War II, Austin gasoline engines were standard in the Bristol until Perkins diesels came to dominate the range in the 1950s. In 1970, Bristol was taken over by Marshall.

1947 Bristol 20
The Bristol crawler had a long career starting around 1930 and featured many engine variations over the years. This 1947 Bristol 20 was powered by an Austin 16 automobile engine.

1947 Bristol 20
The Bristol 20 was powered by the Austin 16 automobile engine and rode on Roadless tracks. The Bristol 20 was followed by the 22, which came with either an Austin A70 or Perkins diesel.

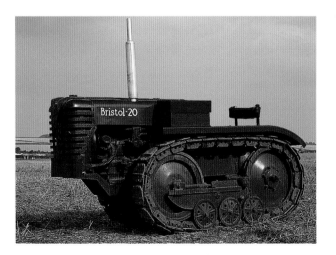

The BEST Oil Tractor made.

Latest Model of 80—100 B.HP. Oil Tractor.

MAXIMUM WHEEL ADHESION.
MINIMUM LENGTH.
EXCELLENT DESIGN.
MASSIVE STRENGTH.
SOUND CONSTRUCTION.

1911 Clayton & Shuttleworth Oil Tractor brochure

Above: This 1911 brochure described Clayton & Shuttleworth as the world's largest maker of steam threshing machinery with 100,000 in use. Clayton & Shuttleworth's 1911 Oil Tractor was a massive four-cylinder machine with 80/100 horsepower. Versions with 45 and 60 horsepower were also available.

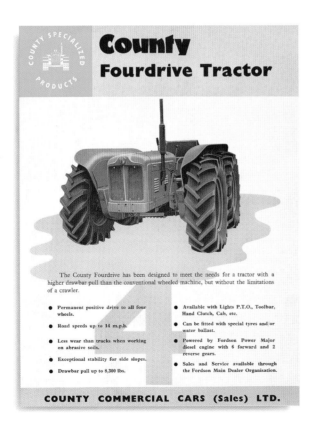

County Fourdrive Tractor

The County Fourdrive has been designed to meet the needs for a tractor with a higher drawbar pull than the conventional wheeled machine, but without the limitations of a crawler.

- Permanent positive drive to all four wheels.
- Road speeds up to 14 m.p.h.
- Less wear than tracks when working on abrasive soils.
- Exceptional stability for side slopes.
- Drawbar pull up to 8,300 lbs.

- Available with Lights P.T.O., Toolbar, Hand Clutch, Cab, etc.
- Can be fitted with special tyres and/or water ballast.
- Powered by Fordson Power Major diesel engine with 6 forward and 2 reverse gears.
- Sales and Service available through the Fordson Main Dealer Organisation.

COUNTY COMMERCIAL CARS (Sales) LTD.

CLAYTON & SHUTTLEWORTH

Clayton & Shuttleworth Ltd. of Lincoln started as steam engineers in 1842 and became important makers of traction engines both for Britain and Central Europe, where the firm was involved with Hungary's HSCS. By 1869, Clayton & Shuttleworth had sold 1,800 steam portables, making it the world's largest producer.

In 1911, the firm launched a tractor with an oil-powered four-cylinder engine behind an automotive-type radiator. The tractor's sheet-metal hood and cab roof featured an extremely advanced design for the time. In 1916, the oil tractor was followed by an equally futuristic gas-kerosene four-cylinder "Chain-Rail" crawler tractor as well as by a 100-horsepower gun tractor similar in style to the American Holt. The 40-horsepower agricultural machine lasted through the 1920s.

In 1929, Clayton & Shuttleworth was bought by Marshall, who particularly wanted the combine harvesters it had been developing.

COUNTY

Founded in 1929, County Commercial Cars Ltd. built most of its success on converting Ford products for specialized roles such as winch work, forestry, peat digging, and load carrying. County started by converting Ford trucks from two to three axles. Beginning in 1948, County turned Fordson Majors into crawlers, followed in 1954 by a version with four equal-sized wheels but still with skid-steering for sugar-cane harvesting. Later in the 1950s, County-modified Fordsons kept the equal-sized-wheel arrangement, but the front pair now steered; in 1965, a forward-control version with a sizeable load space was crafted. After twenty-five years of Ford-based tractor conversions, County had become by far the largest operation of its type, with total sales of 30,000 machines.

When Ford decided to build its own four-wheel-drive tractors in the late 1970s, the business for County and other conversion firms suffered. In 1982, County used Perkins engines in its Ford conversions. County has continued to retain a small presence in the specialist four-wheel-drive tractor market.

1950s County Fourdrive brochure

County's Fourdrive four-wheel-drive tractor had chain drive to the four wheels, steering brakes as on a crawler, and a fourteen-miles-per-hour (22-km/h) top speed.

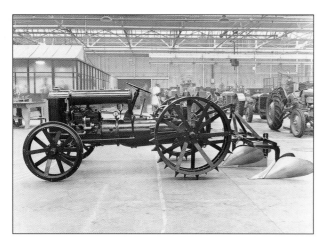

1933 Ferguson-Brown Type A
Above: *The original 1933 Ferguson-Brown tractor with Harry Ferguson's patented plow and three-point hitch. In the background at the Coventry factory is one of the David Brown–built models sandwiched between post–World War II Fergusons TE-20s.*

1947 David Brown Cropmaster
Below: *The Cropmaster could be fitted with a six-speed gearbox and electric starting with its 25/35-horsepower, four-cylinder, wet-liner engine*

DAVID BROWN

Gear makers from 1860 to this day, David Brown of Meltham, Huddersfield, became involved in the production of Irishman Harry Ferguson's first tractors, in 1936. In all, it built 1,350 of the advanced Type A Ferguson-Browns incorporating Ferguson's many patents.

When Henry Ford and Ferguson shook hands on their legendary "Gentleman's Agreement," David Brown decided to stay in the tractor business on its own and supplied many tractors to the British Royal Air Force for aircraft towing. David Brown created two agricultural versions, the VAK-K for kerosene and the VAG-G for gasoline. These farming models had distinctive knee guards and bench seats. In 1947, they were replaced by the improved Cropmaster line, some models featuring six-speed gearboxes. Diesels arrived in 1949.

With the purchase of the makers of Albion implements in the mid-1950s, David Brown offered a full tractor and implement line starting in 1955. Meanwhile, the firm's chairman, David Brown, had come

CROPMASTER

AN EVEN BETTER TRACTOR

FROM A FAMOUS MANUFACTURER

DAVID BROWN

1954 David Brown 30D
Above: *Driver's eye view of the 30D instrument panel, with just oil and amp gauges to worry about.*

1954 David Brown 30D
Below: *David Brown came onto the diesel scene with its Cropmaster and then improved on it with the direct-injection unit in the 30D of 1953–1958. This 30D had a 34-horsepower diesel, although a 30C with a gas/kerosene engine was also available. The tractor is mounted with a matching Albion forage harvester. Owner: Mike Fletcher of Wellington, Great Britain.*

to the public's attention with his acquisition of famed British performance car makers Aston Martin and Lagonda (which later became Ford subsidiaries).

The 100,000th David Brown tractor was made in 1956, and the firm continued to produce sophisticated machines with the most up-to-date hydraulics and transmissions, some of which it also supplied to the American Oliver firm.

In 1972, David Brown was purchased by the American Tenneco firm. The Case and David Brown ranges were then integrated, and the famous British name disappeared in 1983. Through the years, well over half a million David Brown tractors were sold.

1953 David Brown 25C

Left: *David Brown's 25C was a 32-horsepower gasoline tractor, fitted here with a Mil loader. Starting in 1954, David Browns had sophisticated hydraulics with special Traction Control Units. Owner: Mike Fletcher of Wellington, Great Britain.*

1940s David Brown VAKI brochure

Below: *A late-wartime David Brown VAKI with 26/35-horsepower four-cylinder engine. The driver is a Land Army Girl.*

FERGUSON AND MASSEY-FERGUSON

Born in 1884 in Northern Ireland, Harry Ferguson worked on cars, motorcycles, airplanes, and then, from 1914, on farm tractors. He thought it absurd that tractors were built to be heavy, and thus cumbersome, in order to obtain maximum traction. He began work on a weight-transferring drawbar and on plows with automatic depth control, which were made in the United States by Ferguson-Sherman, Inc., of Evansville, Indiana. The two ideas were combined in the 1936 Ferguson-Brown Type A, built with David Brown. The Type A was the first light tractor with sophisticated draft control hydraulics.

Based on a handshake between Ferguson and Henry Ford creating the famous "Gentleman's Agreement," the American Ford firm used Ferguson's ideas in the Ford-Ferguson 9N and 2N tractors. Ford made 306,221 of the revolutionary tractors from 1939 to 1947.

Unfortunately, the relationship turned sour following Henry Ford's death, and Ferguson established production in England of his own Ferguson tractor—which initially bore a suspicious resemblance to the Ford-Ferguson. The Ferguson tractors were built by the makers of Standard cars; in the late 1940s, Ferguson also established a factory in Detroit, Michigan. In 1951, diesel-engined Fergusons were offered.

In 1953, Harry Ferguson, Inc., merged with Canada's Massey-Harris to form Massey-Harris-Ferguson, Ltd., commonly called simply Massey-Ferguson. By 1953, Ferguson had built 339,420 Ferguson tractors. Harry Ferguson had little involvement with Massey-Ferguson, but continued experiments at his own Harry Ferguson Research.

Three-cylinder Perkins diesels were used in Ferguson models after Massey-Harris's takeover; Perkins was acquired by Massey-Ferguson in 1959. Production of Massey-Ferguson tractors continued at Standard's tractor factory, which was acquired by Massey in 1959. The FE35 of 1956 was an important new model, initially distinguished by its gold-painted engine and transmission; in 1957, the FE35 became the gray-and-red MF35. Some tractors were still called Fergusons for select markets.

Harry Ferguson always advocated small, light, frugal, and inexpensive machines, but following his death in 1960, Massey-Ferguson tractors began to move up the horsepower range. A new pressure-controlled

Multipull hitch arrived in 1960.

As happened throughout the industry, safety cabs were standardized in 1970. Early in the 1970s, oil-cooled brakes, six-speed gearboxes, and a pivot-steered four-wheel-drive model with equal-sized wheels were introduced. This for the first time gave Massey-Ferguson a complete line of models. The range subsequently continued to grow until its 1995 acquisition by AGCO, and soon after, the three-millionth Massey-Ferguson was built.

1955 Ferguson TED-20
Above: *The TED-20 featured a 23.9-horsepower tractor vaporizing oil (TVO) version of the Standard 25-horsepower engine. Owner: Brian Whitlock of Yeovil, Great Britain.*

1930s Ferguson-Brown Type A brochure
Right: *An interesting leaflet from Harry Ferguson, Ltd., while based with David Brown, explaining the advantages of Ferguson's ideas.*

THE 'FERGUSON' RIDES ON TOP OF THE SOIL DUE TO LIGHTNESS & EVEN WEIGHT DISTRIBUTION

1955 Ferguson TEF-20
Above: *There are still hundreds of Fergusons at work on small farms in the United Kingdom. The early Fergusons have 122-ci (2.0-liter) engines based on the engines in the Standard Vanguard sedan and the Triumph TR2 sports car.*

1955 Ferguson TEF-20
Left: *A 1955 TEF-20 fitted with a Standard Motor Company 25-horsepower, 122-ci (2.0-liter) diesel. The Ferguson was available with a range of mounted implements for virtually every farm job imaginable. Owner: Brian Whitlock of Yeovil, Great Britain.*

FORDSON

Henry Ford's famous American Fordson tractor was launched in Great Britain in 1917, one year before its introduction in the United States. Starting in 1919, Ford built the Fordson Model F in Cork, Ireland, as well as in Dearborn, Michigan. In 1929, all Fordson production was shifted to Cork, and the improved Model N with a larger engine, bearings, and radiator, and stronger wheels made its debut.

In 1933, all Fordson production was moved to a new factory in Dagenham, England, and Fordsons were exported back to the United States and Canada. With the transfer to England, the Fordson gradually evolved through the 1930s: One of the most obvious changes was a shift from the water washer to the smaller oil-filled air cleaner in 1937. Also in 1937, the general-purpose row-crop Fordson All-Around was launched, intended primarily for the American and Canadian markets.

In 1945, the Fordson E27N Major was unveiled. Although it was mechanically similar to the Model N, it was available with a three-point implement lift. The E27N was offered in gas or tractor vaporizing oil (TVO) models, and a Perkins diesel option was soon available.

In 1952, compact Majors with modern sheet metal arrived, followed by the much smaller Dexta models with 32 brake horsepower. These were all widely exported, and laid the basis for a massive expansion in the Ford of England range in the 1960s. By the mid-1970s, Ford was producing 320 tractors daily, as well as a further 120 tractors daily in Belgium.

In recent years, Ford began making all the diesel engines used by Ford tractor factories in the United States and Great Britain. In 1993, Fiat of Italy bought a controlling interest in Ford tractors, and under its control, New Holland continues to build New Holland Ford tractors.

1939 Fordson Model N Land Utility
Having been made in small numbers at Cork, Ireland, from 1929, around 200,000 Fordsons were produced at Dagenham, England, from 1933 to 1945.

1939 Fordson Model N Land Utility
The Model N Land Utility model brought pneumatic tires to the range in 1935. The tractors were initially fitted with 24-inch (60-cm) wheels, but in 1939, they rode on 28-inch (70-cm) wheels. This Model N featured an oil-bath air cleaner and the engine top end was redesigned for more power by Harry Ricardo. Owner: Dennis Crossman of Walton, Somerset, Great Britain.

1940s Fordson Model N

Above: *The Fordson's Dagenham blue with red trim livery was changed to all orange late in 1937, and then to green in 1940 to make the tractors less vulnerable to German Luftwaffe aircraft during World War II. During the war, Fordson built 94 percent of all the tractors made in Britain. The radiator blind was critical to successful running as the original gas engine was deliberately over-cooled and diesels inherently ran even cooler.*

Left: **1930s Fordson Model N Standard brochure**

1937 Fordson Model N Standard

Facing page: *Painted in the first phase of Dagenham blue with red lettering livery, this Fordson N rode on iron wheels, which were cast at the front and fabricated at the rear with spade lugs. The four-cylinder engine displaced 267 ci (4.37 liters). Owner: Eric Coates of Southampton, Great Britain.*

1950s Fordson Dexta
Above: *The Dexta of 1957–1964 gave Ford a little 32-horse-power model to compete with the Massey-Ferguson 35.*

1952 Fordson Major brochure
Below: *The new Fordson Major appeared in 1952 with either a 220-ci (3.6-liter) four-cylinder diesel or kerosene engine, or a 199-ci (3.26-liter) gasoline engine. The new Major was also available with six forward and two reverse gears.*

1946 Fordson E27N Major

The 1946 E27N used the Model N engine, although it was now fitted with provision for an electric starter. Starting in 1948, hydraulics were available as well as Perkins P6 diesels.

1959 Fordson Dexta and 1962 Fordson Super Major

Above: *The Super Major in the foreground was available with a Ford 44-horsepower, four-cylinder gas engine or Ford 52-horsepower diesel. The little sibling to the Super Major in the background was the Perkins P3-powered Fordson Dexta. To built the Dexta's engine, Ford's foundry supplied cylinder blocks to Perkins. Super Major owner: Jonathan Philip of Looe, Cornwall, Great Britain.*

1964 Fordson New Performance Super Dexta

Left, top: *The Super Dexta was a more powerful replacement for the Dexta. In the United States, it was known as the Ford 2000 Diesel.*

1965 Ford-Northrop 5004

Left, bottom: *County and Roadless are the most familiar names in Ford four-wheel-drive conversions, but the Chaseside Company of Blackburn, Lancashire, also built its Northrop conversions between 1965 and 1967. The Northrop was based on the Ford 5000 skid unit, and many of its features were found on the subsequent Muir-Hill MH 101. Owner: Duke Potter of Swindon, Great Britain.*

GENERAL AND RUSHTON

The General was introduced in 1928 as a straight copy of the Fordson. One of Britain's largest firms, the London General Omnibus Company, which owned the AEC commercial vehicle factory, was involved in building the General. George Rushton, who ran the tractor operation, also had interests in a Ford dealership and soon substituted his name on the General tractors. He also gained AEC's former works when that firm moved from London to Southall.

Rushton's idea was to make 10,000 tractors a year, which was plainly absurd in the light of the 3,000 to 4,000 Fordsons built annually at the time. Also involved in the project was Walter Hill, who had worked at Ford and later was involved with Bristol tractors and Muir-Hill.

For all the high hopes, the business soon collapsed. It was salvaged by Tractors (London) Ltd., who made the little Trusty horticultural tractors and continued building the Rushton in limited quantities through the 1930s.

GLASGOW

The Glasgow tractor of 1919 was an attempt to mass produce an advanced three-wheel-drive tractor. The Glasgow was the brainchild of three Scottish firms—Carmuirs Iron Foundry, John Wallace & Sons, and D. L. Motors—who joined forces to build the tractor at a vast former munitions factory at Cardonald near Glasgow, Scotland. Like earlier tractors of this layout—including the Rose and others in the United States and the Saunderson in Britain—it was not a commercial success, largely due to its complexity and the arrival of the far less expensive Fordson. Glasgow tractor production ended in 1924.

"The machine simply bristles with innovations"
—Country Life

"GLASGOW"
Farm Tractor

The positive drive on all three wheels gives greater tractive adhesion, obviates slipping and skidding and the tendency to tip up. The "GLASGOW" can turn in a very small circle. The drawbar can be altered in position laterally by a lever at the driver's seat and a self-lift plough can be operated by a pedal instead of the driver having to steer with one hand and manipulate a rope with the other.

25 b.h.p.   Price £450

Write for Illustrated Descriptive Booklet C2 to the Sole Concessionaires for the British Empire (excepting Canada):

BRITISH·MOTOR·TRADING
CORPORATION LTD
20, 21, 22, KING ST., ST. JAMES', LONDON, S.W. 1
GLASGOW OFFICE: 27, ROYAL EXCHANGE SQUARE

1920s Glasgow advertisement
Above: *Bird's eye view of the neat and compact three-wheel-drive Glasgow. The innovative tractor was powered by a 27-horsepower Waukesha engine, although some had Scottish-built sleeve-valve units.*

1928 General T34
Below: *The General tractor at the end of a plowing test marathon. George Rushton stands second from left.*

1902–1903 Ivel
Dan Albone's Ivel had a two-cylinder, horizontally opposed, 20-horsepower gasoline engine and single forward and reverse gears. It was the first light and simple farm tractor to sell in quantity, and was built in the United Kingdom and the United States.

MARSHALL
1930 DIESEL TRACTOR
RATING 15/30 H.P.
MODEL "E."
Manufactured by
MARSHALL, SONS & Co., Ltd.
Engineers,
GAINSBOROUGH, ENGLAND

Uses heavy oil far cheaper in price than petrol and cuts ploughing costs down to
FIVE PENCE PER ACRE

1930 Marshall Model E brochure
Unlike the contemporary and similar-looking Lanz Bulldog, the 1930 single-cylinder Marshall was a true cold-start diesel. The 15/30-horsepower engine's bore and stroke measured a massive 8x10.5 inches (200x262.5 mm).

IVEL

The Ivel, named after a river in Bedfordshire, was the work of champion bicyclist Dan Albone. He received a patent in 1902 for mounted implements with the necessary rotating power provided from the tractor, a pioneering power takeoff (PTO). In 1903, Albone began production of the Ivel in Biggleswade. The three-wheel lightweight was powered by a two-cylinder 8-horsepower gasoline engine.

After Albone's premature death in 1906, the Ivel changed little in appearance to the end of production in 1921. Ivel Agricultural Motors also imported the smallest Hart-Parr tractor models into Great Britain during World War I.

MARSHALL AND FOWLER

The Marshall Sons & Company of Gainsborough and Fowler of Leeds were famous old names from the days of steam traction. Both firms built ranges of gas tractors before joining forces in 1947.

Marshall made internal-combustion-engined tractors from 1908. In 1929, the firm developed a single-cylinder two-stroke full-diesel tractor, which evolved through to the mid-1950s as the venerable Field Marshall.

Fowler made a variety of tractors over the years, including its well-known winch-plowing steam engines and its Gyrotillers of the 1920s and 1930s, which had rotating tines for large-scale cultivation and came in various sizes up to 200 brake horsepower. Fowler built a crawler version of the Field Marshall under its own name and also made larger crawlers through to the 1970s.

Both Marshall and Fowler have led rather a checkered existence since then, but both have produced some interesting tractors, including the Marshall MP6 powered by a Leyland six-cylinder engine. Marshall's tractor business was later acquired by Leyland Motors.

In the 1980s, Marshall broke away from Leyland and acquired both the Leyland and Aveling-Marshall tractor operations. Marshall continued limited production through the 1990s.

1948 Marshall Series II Contractors Model

Above: *Like the Marshall Model M and the Lanz Bulldog, but unlike the original Marshalls, the Series II had its radiator placed at the side to avoid damage. This tractor is fitted with Marshall's own winch that was suitable for various duties including maneuvering a threshing machine, which it could then run all day on five gallons (18 liters) of diesel fuel at maximum revs of a mere 750 rpm. Owner: Malcolm Goddard of Tiverton, Great Britain.*

1938 Marshall Model M brochure

Left: *The Model M was launched in 1938 and promoted as "All British." The large diesel engine featured a 6.5x9-inch (162.5x225-mm) bore and stroke.*

1955 Marshall IIIA
Left: *Owner Malcolm Goddard goes through the cold-starting procedure: A lighted wick is inserted in the cylinder head; a swing on the flywheel would then normally set the engine in motion, although some used special cartridges to force the piston through its first stroke.*

1950s Marshall MP6
Below, top: *The great single-cylinder Marshalls ended with a final batch in the late 1950s. They were joined in 1954 by the large and expensive 70-horsepower, six-cylinder, Leyland-engined MP6, which took two years to reach series production. The vast majority of the approximately 200 built were exported.*

1948 Marshall Series II Contractors Model
Below, bottom: *Christopher Shere aboard Malcolm Goddard's Marshall Series II.*

Nuffield and Leyland

In 1948, Lord Nuffield—formerly William Morris, Britain's largest mass-producer of cars—made a noble attempt to break into the world of tractors with his Nuffield machine, made by his Nuffield Mechanisations firm that had built military vehicles during World War II. Produced at a massive war materiel factory in Birmingham, his tractor featured sophisticated hydraulic systems, a five-speed gearbox, and some useful diesel expertise, gained initially from the Swiss Saurer firm.

Nuffield's orange tractors earned a good reputation and became popular in the 1950s. Offered in various sizes, they lasted through to the late 1969 takeover of Morris Motors, Austin, and the other members of the British Motor Corporation by Leyland Motors to create British Leyland Motor Corporation. The blue-painted Leyland tractor range continued at a new Scottish factory.

In 1968, Leyland acquired the Aveling-Barford construction machinery maker. Aveling-Barford had been created in 1933 from the Aveling-Porter firm following a merger with Barford and Perkins, when Frank Perkins left to make diesel engines. Leyland also adopted Marshall's crawlers, calling them the Aveling-Marshall.

In 1982, Leyland decided to concentrate on its core business. Marshall broke away from the Leyland concern and later acquired both the Leyland and Aveling-Marshall tractor operations.

1949 Nuffield Universal M4
Below, top: *Paul Cluyas's father bought this Universal M4 new in 1949. After it had worked for forty years, Paul, of Cornwall, Great Britain, restored the Nuffield.*

1967 Nuffield-Bray 4/65
Below, bottom: *The Bray Construction Equipment Company Ltd. Of Feltham, Middlesex, built its first farm tractor in 1961, the Centaur. The Bray had two-way plows mounted at each end. These were superseded by Nuffield-based models, such as the 1967 example shown here, built under the aegis of Pivot-Steer loader maker Matbro, which acquired Bray in the 1960s. This Nuffield-based Bray four-wheel drive has been uprated from a four-cylinder 65-horsepower to a six-cylinder BMC 103-horsepower diesel. Owner: Clarence DeLacour of Barnstable, North Devon, Middlesex, Great Britain.*

Petter

The Petter was remarkable for being a compact, oil-powered traction engine available as early as 1896–1897. In 1903, Petter offered its forward-control Petter's Patent Agricultural Vehicle with a 12-horsepower tube-ignition engine and three forward gears.

Afterwards, Petter concentrated mostly on barn engines and implements, but created an inexpensive semi-diesel three-wheeler in 1915. Petter soon afterward took over production of the Maskell motor plow. Petter's name lives on with the Lister-Petter engines, while a different branch of the firm gave birth to Westland aircraft and helicopters.

Ransomes

Starting with steam traction engines, Ransomes moved on to offer gas tractors from 1902 to 1904 that resembled Spartan motor cars with specially cleated iron drive wheels, after which the company became best known for its plows. Ransomes made a range of small horticultural tractors on Roadless tracks from the 1930s to the 1960s. Recent products have been primarily for lawn care. The American Textron firm, maker of Jacobsen mowers, bought Ransomes in 1997.

1926 Saunderson Universal brochure

Below, top: *The Saunderson was a contemporary of the Ivel, and this Universal model changed little in appearance for twenty years up to this late example of 1926. It had a transverse 20-horsepower, two-cylinder engine and was also offered in France as the SCEMIA.*

1959 Ransomes MG6

Below, bottom: *Ransomes was a famous old name in the agricultural machinery business, and the firm's 8-horsepower, single-cylinder diesel MG6 carried on the tradition. These little horticultural crawlers initially featured gasoline engines; they were made with Roadless tracks starting in 1936. In 1997, the U.S. makers of Jacobsen lawn tractors bought the business.*

ROADLESS

Roadless Traction adapted Ford and other makes of truck and tractor for special agricultural work. From the 1940s through the 1960s, Roadless concentrated on Fords, first building half-track tractors and then four-wheel drives.

Other familiar names in the conversion field were Northrop and Muir-Hill.

SAUNDERSON

The Saunderson tractor was the work of Herbert Percy Saunderson of Bedford, Bedfordshire. The prototype was believed to have been built in 1896 and production to have commenced in 1902. After building some big two-wheeled motor plows, and even a tractor with three driven wheels that was entered at the 1908 Winnipeg plowing contest in Canada, the firm settled down to craft tractors with a layout resembling the later Crossmotor Case.

In the 1920s, Saunderson launched a streamlined and inexpensive Light Tractor, but it made few inroads against the new Fordson. Saunderson eked out a limited livelihood into the late 1920s with its traditional 25-horsepower Model G, which had been unveiled in 1912. In its last years, Saunderson and Model G production was under the control of engine makers Crossley.

TURNER

The Turner Manufacturing Company of Wolverhampton made various cars and light commercial vehicles during its long existence. In 1949, the firm introduced its Yeoman of England tractor, powered by Turner's own V-4 diesel engine, which produced 32/40 horsepower. The tractor proved to be popular with contractors and large-scale farmers.

VICKERS

Vickers has long been a massive engineering group making everything from warships to today's Rolls-Royce cars. Starting in 1927, it made large tractors inspired by American models; the tractors were built principally for the Australian market. With competition in the tractor field and a call to arms as World War II loomed, Vickers halted tractor production in 1933.

After its experience making tanks for the World War II effort, Vickers made a brief attempt to combat Caterpillar with a range of Rolls-Royce–powered crawlers.

1950s Turner Yeoman of England advertisement
The 40-horsepower Yeoman of England was fast and powerful, but proved too expensive for all but contractors.

1957 Vickers Vikon brochure
The Vickers Vikon crawler was powered by a brawny 495-ci (8.1-liter) Rolls-Royce four-cylinder diesel; with supercharging, the Vikon boasted 142 belt horsepower. The Vickers had five forward and four reverse gears.

ITALY

taly's Fiat, SAME, Lamborghini, and OM are
all familiar tractor makers, but it often seems
that just about every agricultural town in the
north of the country had its own workshop
producing tractors. These were mostly compact four-wheel-drive multi-purpose vehicles, often with some sort of load-carrying space. Some had become important in
their region, such as Pasquali, Goldoni,
Antonio Carraro, and Ferrari (not connected with the exotic-car maker), which
all crafted sophisticated tractors incorporating features one would not expect
to find in a 100-horsepower tractor, let
alone a model with a mere 15 or 35 horsepower. There are
also some little-known makers of full ranges of tractors, such as Agrifull Toselli, as well as
lots of modified imports, and even some Fordsons built in Bologna from the years shortly
before and after World War II.

1954 Landini L25
Facing page: *The stylish Landini L25 was rated at 25/35 horsepower. Owner: Jim Thomas.*

1930 Fiat 700A poster
Above: *This brochure image showed the Fiat tractor's "il lavoro di una giornata," or "the work of one day."*

A few pioneering firms made tractors early on, such as Alfa Romeo (1920–1935), Baroncelli (1912–1914), Breda (1920–1950), Bubba (1925–1956), Motomeccanica (1920s–1958), and Orsi (1930–1956).

CARRARO

The firms of Carraro SpA and Antonio Carraro in Campodarsego have made complementary models since the mid-1950s. Antonio Carraro concentrated on small-horsepower tractors finished in blue and orange while Carraro SpA made larger models finished in red and olive.

Carraro SpA models began with the firm's own air-cooled diesels but gained Perkins engines in the mid-1970s before a reversion to air cooling with Deutz diesels. Synchro transmissions had sixteen forward and four reverse gears. Along with its crawlers, the firm made a specialty of four-wheel drives, becoming the third largest Italian producer in the early 1970s. It also supplied its epicyclic-reduction front axles to other tractor makers, notably France's Renault. Renault has also bought some complete Carraros to sell in France under its own colors.

1932 Alfa Romeo crawler
Above: *The Alfa Romeo crawler was designed to replace two oxen with its 10/15-horsepower, 104-ci (1.7-liter) engine. It had six forward gears and steering clutches worked by wheel. This French brochure hyphenated the Italian firm's name.*

1927 Cassani
Below: *Remarkable for being a full diesel, the 1927 Cassani had a gigantic two-cylinder, 775-ci (12.7-liter) engine.*

1960s SAME 480 DTB Ariete
Above: *The Ariete was powered by an air-cooled, four-cylinder, 305-ci (5.0-liter) diesel.*

1960s SAME 480 DTB Ariete
Below: *"Ariete" stood for "Ram," and SAME's late-1960s Ariete tractor was indeed a potent machine. Its engine fathered 80 horsepower, and combined with its four-wheel drive and eight-speed gearbox, it had the power to tackle almost any job.*

Cassani and SAME

Francesco Cassani's 1927 tractor was the world's first diesel-powered tractor outside Germany, the country where the diesel was invented. The Cassani's two-cylinder horizontal 775-ci (12.7-liter) engine developed 40 horsepower at 450 rpm. A small number were built up to 1932. Cassani then concentrated on fuel-injection systems, but in 1936 offered a little 10-horsepower gas-engined three-wheeled tractor. Cassani-badged tractors continued to about 1960.

Cassani established SAME (Società Anònima Motori Endothermic) in the late 1930s and built thirty-three tractors between 1942 and 1948. SAME launched a new range in 1950 of 20-horsepower twin-cylinder tractors. From 1951, most SAME tractors were powered by a range of one-, two-, three-, and four-cylinder modular air-cooled diesel units.

In 1951, SAME took the brave step of offering four-wheel drive on virtually all its models. By 1972, 33,392 four-wheel-drive SAMEs were in use in Italy, well ahead of Fiat with 20,144 in the number two spot for four-wheel drives.

In 1960, the SAME 240 debuted with a new type

of hydraulic depth control with sensing on the lower link arms rather than top links. SAME then created the unique load-carrying and -hauling SAMECAR with forward control, but the vehicle was not a success, and production ended in 1969.

By 1977, SAME had sold a total of 213,258 tractors since its founding and was producing 20,000 new tractors annually with the distinctive model names Delfino, Buffalo, Tauro, Leopardo, and Centauro gracing the orange machines. By 1981, eighteen SAME models were offered in thirty-two versions with power ratings from 30 to 150 horsepower, and annual sales reached 30,000 tractors.

In 1972, SAME acquired Lamborghini's tractor business and was supplying parts to the Swiss Hürlimann firm, which it subsequently took over. Since then, SAME has continued to expand, purchasing Deutz-Fahr of Germany in 1995.

1931 Fiat tractor lineup
Photographed in an Italian field in 1931, from left to right, a 1925 Fiat 703B, 1927 Fiat 700N, and a rival Fordson, which was soon to be assembled at Bologna by Ford Italiana SpA. Fiat's 703B was powered by a 378-ci (6.2-liter) engine whereas the 700N featured a 201-ci (3.3.-liter) engine.

FIAT

Fiat was Europe's largest producer of tractors even before it acquired controlling interest in Ford's tractor division in 1991 to create New Holland's line of tractors.

Founded in 1899 by Giovanni Agnelli and based in Turin, Fiat was originally an acronym for Fabbrica Italiana di Automobili Torino. The firm's first farm tractor was the 702 model developed in 1918 based on World War I gun tractors. The 702 was powered by a 380-ci (6.23-liter) overhead-valve engine. Fiat made 263 in 1919 and went on to produce more than 2,000 of the type. By 1929, Fiat was selling more than 1,000 farm tractors annually.

After a depressed economic period in the 1930s selling only a few hundred smaller tractors each year, Fiat was successful with its 700C crawler starting in 1932. Later in the decade, Fiat adopted the Boghetto system to enable crawlers to start on petrol and then run on diesel, an idea also employed on International crawlers.

Sales finally increased in 1949 with 1,832 tractors produced, sparked by Fiat's launch of its successful

compact, 18-horsepower 600 model, followed by small diesel-engined types in 1953. In 1955, Fiat began building numerous four-wheel-drive models.

Tractor output boomed to 22,637 in 1959, 55,735 in 1968, 78,934 in 1976, and 116,000 in 1995. The 1.5 millionth Fiat tractor was made in 1980. Meanwhile, Fiat exports of 504 tractors in 1948 grew to 15,488 in 1955, and more than 50,000 for the first time in 1976. Fiats were sold in the United States by forage equipment maker Hesston, a FiatAgri subsidiary since 1977.

Fiat forged links in the early 1950s with SIMCA of France, which made Fiat cars and then French SOMECA tractors based on Fiat designs. By the 1970s, other overseas licensees and producers of Fiat tractors included Uzina Tractorul Brasov (UTB) of Romania, Turk Traktor of Turkey, Tovarna of Yugoslavia, and Fiat Concord of Argentina.

In a change of direction in 1974, Fiat joined Allis-Chalmers in creating the Fiat-Allis construction machinery range of crawler tractors (made in Brazil, the United States, and Italy), wheel loaders (the United States and England), excavators (Italy and Brazil), graders and scrapers (the United States). Starting in 1979, Fiat embarked on another North American link, selling large four-wheel-drive tractors from Canada's Versatile in Europe under the Fiat name.

Over the years, Fiat has acquired numerous smaller tractor makers, bringing their designs and models into the Fiat fold. In 1933, Fiat bought veteran truck and tractor maker OM, which then operated in close conjunction with Fiat's Società Ligure Piemontese Automobili (SPA) subsidiary. Both OM and SPA made four-wheel-drive tractors inspired by the earlier Pavesi tractor, which Fiat had purchased in the early 1920s and made for military purposes since 1926.

In 1975, Fiat acquired the combine line of Laverda of Breganze. Laverda built auxiliary engines for farm machinery from 1935 and other farm implements before venturing into motorcycles. In 1984, Fiat purchased the French firm Braud, the world leader in self-propelled grape harvesting equipment.

1957 Fiat 18 La Piccola
Above, top: *Fiat's La Piccola, or "The Little One," was the firm's smallest tractor. Some 20,000 were sold from 1956 to 1958.*

1958 Fiat tractor range
Above, bottom: *The Fiat range in 1958 including a wide variety of crawlers and wheeled two- and four-wheel-drive vineyard and construction models. Several Fiat tractors continued to wear the OM badge on their grille.*

1950 Lamborghini

Top: *Lamborghini started by making tractors from surplus World War II materiel. This 1950 example has a 40-horsepower British Morris-Commercial six-cylinder engine.*

1920s Landini

Center: *Based on the firm's earlier stationary engines, this was one of Landini's first tractors. It was launched in the mid-1920s with a hopper-cooled, 30-horsepower, hot-bulb engine.*

1930s Landini

Bottom: *By the late 1930s, the Landini had been refined into a well-built tractor. It now featured dynamo lighting and a 40-horsepower engine topped by a prominent air cleaner.*

LAMBORGHINI

Unlike the compact Ferrari tractors made by an Italian firm unconnected with the famous car company of the same name, Lamborghini cars and tractors were both created by the same man, Ferruccio Lamborghini.

Lamborghini started building tractors in 1947 using military surplus vehicle parts. He soon managed to buy 1,000 Morris six-cylinder gasoline engines to serve as tractor powerplants. When these were all used up, Lamborghini's orange-painted tractors switched to German MWM and English Perkins diesels before the firm developed its own air-cooled units in 1954.

After the successful arrival of Lamborghini oil burners, ventilation equipment, and then, in 1963, exotic cars, Ferruccio Lamborghini sold the tractor business to SAME in 1972. He had grown nervous about the tractor field since the collapse of a Bolivian government order in the 1960s for 5,000 tractors.

SAME was soon building about 5,000 white-painted wheeled and crawler Lamborghinis annually. These had two-, three-, four-, or six-cylinder air-cooled engines and three-range, four-speed synchro gearboxes that had evolved from the Lamborghini transmissions of the early 1950s.

In 1992, AGCO-White bought four hundred Lamborghinis in the 75- to 115-horsepower range for distribution in the United States.

LANDINI

Giovanni Landini opened a machine shop in 1884 to produce agricultural machinery before developing steam engines in 1911 and portable internal-combustion engines in 1917. Giovanni died in 1924, and his sons took over the business, launching in 1925 a 30-horsepower *testa calda*, or hot-bulb, single-cylinder tractor based on the firm's earlier portable gas engine. The tractor's power output increased to 40 horsepower and then 50 horsepower in the 1930s. Landini sold 900 tractors by 1934, when 250 workers were building four daily.

A diesel version was offered from 1958, but large, lumbering single-cylinder machines were by then outdated—even if the Landini's original three forward gears had now increased to eight—so from 1959, Landini began to use three- and four-cylinder Perkins diesels, which Landini built under license. By 1960, Landini had 500 employees building twenty tractors daily.

Landini joined Canada's Massey-Ferguson group

1930s Landini Super L poster
The power of Landini's 1930s Super L was strikingly displayed in this advertising poster. The Super L was powered by a strong 749-ci (12.2-liter) engine.

in 1960, which also included Perkins. Henceforth, Landini tractors boasted a new blue livery, and a range of crawlers was developed for marketing in the colors of either Landini or Massey. In 1962, Landini launched a line of yellow industrial crawlers; from these models, a whole range of earthmovers made by Massey-Ferguson ICM at a new factory outside Rome was developed in 1968.

Landini's farm tractors were restyled in 1969. In 1971, Landini offered its first six-cylinder models; in 1977, the sixes exceeded the 100-horsepower mark for the first time. Output reached seventy-five wheeled tractors per day by the late 1970s, as well as production of front drive axles for Massey. In the 1990s, Landini is still supplying Massey-Ferguson with some of its smaller specialist models such as vineyard tractors, and Landini tractors are distributed in some markets by AGCO.

1954 Landini L25

Above: *By 1954, single-cylinder hot-bulb tractors were running out of time as technology outpaced the old tried-and-true design. The Landini L25 was relatively unusual, even in its homeland, because most farms were too small to support such a large and expensive machine, hastening the tractor's demise. Owner: Jim Thomas.*

1954 Landini L25

Left: *Flywheel view of the Landini, which operated best between 350 and 750 rpm. Cylinder capacity was 262 ci (4.3 liters). Owner: Jim Thomas.*

OM

Pioneering truck maker OM (Officine Meccaniche) of Brescia began building its T/240 farm tractors in 1927. The T/240 was powered by a horizontal, hot-bulb single-cylinder engine.

In 1937, OM took over Italiano Macchine Agricole di Suzzara, which had been founded in 1878 to build farm carts, later crafting increasingly complex machinery, including CIMAC tractors starting in 1919.

OM was acquired by Fiat in 1933, and worked with Fiat's SPA to build four-wheel-drive tractors. In the late 1960s, OM was still making about 5,000 wheeled and crawler tractors and loaders annually. OM-badged tractors continued to about 1970 .

Pavesi

Ugo Pavesi created Italy's first farm tractor, with rear-wheel drive, around 1911. Working with Giulio Tolotti, Pavesi produced the Pavesi-Tolotti *Tipo* A and *Tipo* B tractors for military and agricultural uses in the early 1920s. Initially powered by a flat twin-cylinder engine, the Pavesi P4 was an ingenious pivot-steered four-wheel drive. These were made by Motomeccanica before Fiat acquired Pavesi in the early 1920s.

The substitution of four-cylinder engines resulted in increasingly large Fiat/SPA Pavesi tractors up to World War II. Pavesi tractors were also built in France, Britain, Sweden, and Hungary.

1920 OM

OM was renowned for its reliable machines, proven by this 1920 tractor still at work as a dockyard shunter in the famous harbor of Genoa, Italy, in the mid-1950s.

1956 OM 45R

Following the takeover by Fiat, OM tractors continued to be produced, still bearing the OM logo on the front. This 45R model features a Manuel Selene four-wheel-drive conversion.

SWEDEN

〜✦〜

Sweden has brought the world Avance, Bolinder-Munktell, Volvo, Bofors, and a few lesser-known makes of tractors. Most were well-engineered tractors, usually from long-established engineering firms.

1966 Bolinder-Munktell BM350
Facing page: *Bolinder-Munktell's BM350 was a large tractor, weighing 3 tons (2,700 kg). Owner: J. U. D. Putten of Deurne, the Netherlands.*

1951 Volvo T22/23
Above: *The T22/23 had a 122-ci (2.0-liter) four-cylinder engine based on the firm's famous car powerplant.*

AVANCE

The Avance was a two-cylinder, hot-bulb-engined tractor available from about 1917. The two-cycle motor was prone to break its crankshaft, but final versions sold in Australia in 1928 by McDonald as the Imperial had better, four-bearing engines. The Avance tractor later evolved into the Bofors tractor in the early 1930s.

BOFORS

Bofors was better known for its guns, but the firm was also the producer of a workmanlike 25/40-horsepower vertical two-cylinder crude-oil tractor in the early 1930s. This was based on the similar Avance tractor available from 1917.

1933 Bofors

Left: *Famous for its armaments production, the Bofors factory offered this 25/40-horsepower, two-cylinder, two-stroke machine in 1933.*

1910s Avance

Below: *The Avance tractor appeared at the time of World War I and was subsequently exported widely.*

BOLINDER-MUNKTELL AND VOLVO

Founded in 1832, Munktell of Eskilstuna built Sweden's first railroad locomotive in 1853, nearly 6,000 portable steam engines from 1853 through 1921, and the country's first internal-combustion-engined tractors starting in 1913. These were 30-horsepower, eight-ton (7,200-kg) monsters, although more compact models appeared in the years between the two world wars, some powered by Bolinder's hot-bulb engines. Bolinder had made internal-combustion engines since 1893 in Stockholm. The two firms merged in 1932 and were taken over by Volvo AG of Göteborg in 1950.

Under Volvo's direction, a new series of one-, two-, three-, four-, and six-cylinder direct-injection diesel engines was introduced in 1953, for use with trucks, tractors, and other purposes. BM's first forestry tractors debuted in 1957. In the 1960s, Volvo tractors were made in Finland by Fiskars.

In 1973, the old corporate names were condensed in the BM Volvo range of tractors, including some unusual pivot-steered, four-wheel-drive, load-carrying agricultural and forestry types based on the six-wheel-drive dump truck developed by BM in 1964. Between 1950 and 1975, 230,000 BM Volvo tractors were sold.

An ingenious feature of the later BM tractors was a modular cab with hydrostatic control linkages that could be removed by detaching simple rubber isolators and couplings. Starting in the mid-1950s, Volvo was an early advocate of turbocharging, although turbos were not widely used on tractors for ten years. Early in the 1970s, Volvo entered a joint component development program with International Harvester and began to use Perkins diesels in tractors.

In 1979, Volvo and Valmet of Finland merged their tractor businesses. Volvo also went on to link its construction machinery division with the makers of Michigan loaders and Euclid dump trucks in the VME Group.

1913 Munktell

Above: *The first Munktell tractor of 1913 was a massive, prairie-busting type of machine with its 30-horsepower engine mounted over the driving wheels.*

1950 Bolinder-Munktell BM10

Below: *Bolinder-Munktell's BM10 was popular in Scandinavia and France. The tractor was compact at 64 inches (160 cm) wide and 102 inches (255 cm) long. The 1950 BM10 had a two-cylinder, two-stroke, semi-diesel engine that developed 14/20 horsepower and had five forward gears. Owner: David Hunt.*

1966 Bolinder-Munktell BM350
The BM350 arrived on the scene in 1960; this particular tractor was built for the Swedish Army in 1966. The BM350 had a 232-ci (3.8-liter) three-cylinder diesel that created 51/56 horsepower.

1966 Bolinder-Munktell BM350
The BM350 had a two-range, five-speed gearbox and was capable of 17.5 miles per hour (28 km/h). Its larger, BM470 sibling had four cylinders of the same 232-ci (3.8-liter) dimensions and developed 61/70 horsepower.

LE DERNIER MODÈLE DE LA NOUVELLE GAMME
DE **3 TRACTEURS DIESEL**

TYPE
BM 230
DE **30** CV. ★ **2** CYL.

ENDURANT ET ECONOMIQUE - DE CLASSE INTERNATIONALE

BOLINDER-MUNKTELL

1950s Bolinder-Munktell BM230
Right: *After World War II, Bolinder-Munktell offered the two-cylinder, full-diesel BM230. Three of its five forward gears had synchromesh.*

UNITED STATES
of AMERICA

Farm tractors were first developed and put to work in significant numbers in the United States. Some 4,500 gasoline-powered tractors were made in the United States in 1910; 29,670 in 1916; and 203,000 in 1920, by which time nearly half were in the 20 to 22 horsepower range. Hundreds of different tractor makers appeared on the American scene, and Henry Ford, who had long yearned for the mechanization of agriculture, unveiled his Fordson. Ford's assembly lines produced 30,000 tractors in 1918 with a target of 100,000 for 1919.

1930s Deere Model AW
Facing page: *The wide-front AW was a version of John Deere's most popular pre–World War II model, the A. The A started production in 1934 with 16/23.5 horsepower and lasted through to 1952 with several power increases.*

1930 Fordson brochure
Above: *Although this Fordson catalog dates from around 1930, the cover illustration shows an early ladder-side radiator and six-spoked rear-wheel Model F.*

American farmers were bewildered by the speed of progress. In 1915, 10,000 turned up at a tractor demonstration in Champaign, Illinois; at the same time, a national survey of those farmers that had purchased a machine reported that nearly half had been stranded with a defective tractor for an annual average of five days. By 1918, half of the American farmers surveyed said that tractors gave better plowing results than horses, although all agreed that the tractor's 7-inch (17.5-cm) instead of the horse's 5½-inch (13.75-cm) furrow was an important benefit.

The mechanization of American farms had only just begun, however. There was still only an average of one tractor for every forty farms in Missouri in 1919, for example, so there were tremendous possibilities for manufacturers if they could reduce tractor prices and improve reliability.

Beyond the American horizon, there was also a huge global market hungering for tractors. Of the tens of thousands of tractors built by American firms by 1917, only 34,371 were in use on American farms; tractors were also being shipped by the thousands to farmers from Russia to South Africa to Argentina.

Mass production of fewer models in greater quantities was the way forward—and marked the end of hundreds of hopeful factories. The University of Nebraska's Department of Agricultural Engineering found that only 15.4 percent of the tractors it tested in 1920 lived up to the manufacturer's claims. The figure improved dramatically to 40 percent in 1921 and 80 percent in 1922 as tractors were refined. Henceforth, the Nebraska Tractor Test became the yardstick of the industry—and increased the farming community's confidence in mechanized horsepower.

The Nebraska tests also helped standardize power ratings: The rating of an 18/30-horsepower tractor indicated 18 drawbar and 30 belt pulley horsepower.

By the dawn of the 1920s, tractors were becoming more powerful, capable, and elaborate. The sale of single-cylinder machines halved in 1920 as larger tractors took their place. Pioneering monobloc four-cylinders temporarily returned to bi-bloc castings at many tractor firms in an effort to increase reliability and simplify maintenance. Six-cylinder tractors appeared on the scene, but many of their promoters were under-capitalized and soon went out of business.

With all of these developments, the 1920s marked the beginning of a recognizable American tractor industry. The big names became bigger as the market

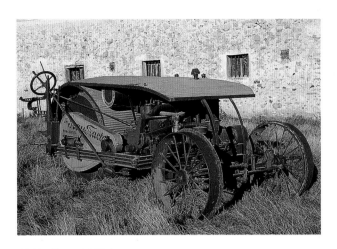

1917 Gray 18/36
The Gray Tractor Company of Minneapolis made drum-drive tractors with two wide rollers set close together for maximum grip. This is the firm's 1917 Waukesha-powered 18/36 model. Pierre Bouillé of Meaux, France.

expanded and many of the smaller firms with a worthwhile product were absorbed by the front-runners.

In the years between the two world wars, just about every development seen on modern tractors was pioneered. All-wheel drive was being experimented with at the end of the nineteenth century and was first used on the 30-, 60-, and 90-horsepower Rose tractor from the Rose Manufacturing Company of San Jose, California, in 1907. Pneumatic tires were first seen on a Fordson in 1921 and soon became available on virtually all makes; 14 percent of all tractors sold in 1935 were fitted with tires increasing to 95 percent in 1940. Other developments included diesel engines in the 1930s; cabs on a few machines; mechanical, and then hydraulic, implement lifts (the Earthmaster tractor from Earthmaster Farm Equipment of Burbank, California, had hydraulics around 1950); and multi-range transmissions. The tractor industry had standardized power takeoff (PTO) shafts at 540 rpm in 1923; by 1958, secondary PTO shafts revolving at 1000 rpm became common.

Since the end of World War II, most tractor developments have focused on increased power, better traction, ease of operation, and comfort. Easy-change gearshifts, often with an epicyclic element, became widespread in the 1950s, as did the use of turbochargers (first tested at Nebraska in 1961 on the Allis-Chalmers D-19), disc brakes, and power steering. The American farm tractor had come a long way.

1920s Allis-Chalmers 20/35

Above: *The biggest Allis-Chalmers in the 1920s was the rare 20/35 with its 461-ci (7.6-liter) engine developing up to 45 horsepower.*

1920s Rumely OilPull 12/20

Left: *The famous Rumely OilPull displays some of its virtues and explains that oil instead of water was the ideal cooling medium.*

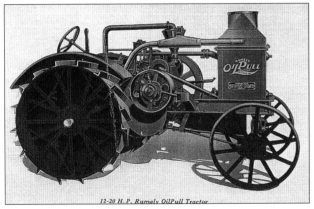

12-20 H. P. Rumely OilPull Tractor

ALLIS-CHALMERS

With a classic agricultural background in flour-milling machinery and factory equipment in the nineteenth century, the Allis-Chalmers Company of Milwaukee, Wisconsin, entered the tractor market in 1914. Its first big seller was the 18/30 produced from 1919 with a four-cylinder engine and conventional layout.

Allis-Chalmers expanded by buying other implement and tractor makers, including the Monarch Tractor Company of Watertown, Wisconsin, producers of the Monarch crawlers, and the famous Advance-

Rumely Thresher Company of LaPorte, Indiana, renowned for its legendary OilPull tractor line.

During the 1930s, Allis-Chalmers had a best-selling tractor in its Models U and UC, originally developed by A-C for a co-operative named the United Tractor and Equipment Company of Chicago, Illinois. By the late 1930s, Allis-Chalmers had captured 13 percent of the American tractor market.

The lightweight Model B of 1937 at $495 brought Allis quality to horticulturists and smaller farms while, at the other end of the scale, the firm's crawlers gained

Detroit diesel engines in 1940. Allis was always an in-novator; For example, the first turbocharged tractor tested at Nebraska was an A-C D-19, in 1961.

Allis-Chalmers became well known to British farmers as a result of the American Lend-Lease Act during World War II, and the familiar orange machines entered production there. In 1959, A-C bought the French tractor firm Vendeuvre, and Allis tractors went into production in France.

After recent links with Deutz of Germany and Fiat of Italy, Allis-Chalmers's tractor interests were acquired by the Allis-Gleaner Company (AGCO) of Duluth, Georgia, which in 1997 also controlled Canada's Massey-Ferguson, America's White, and Germany's Fendt.

1940s Allis-Chalmers WD
Above: *The WD Allis-Chalmers was built from 1948 to 1953, and reached serial number 131,273, providing some idea of its popularity. This WD works with a matching Allis-Chalmers Type 90 combine.*

1940s Allis-Chalmers WC
Right: *Jim Todahl demonstrates a 1950 Allis-Chalmers bale loader powered by the PTO of his Allis-Chalmers row-crop WC. The WC was built from 1933 to 1948 and featured a four-cylinder engine with a "square" bore and stroke of 4 inches (100 mm).*

1941 Allis-Chalmers WF

Above: *The WF was the standard version of the WC row-crop tractor. The WF model was produced 1938 to 1951, and a Lend-Lease example was driven in the Land Army in England during World War II by author Nick Baldwin's mother.*

1939 Allis-Chalmers M brochure

Left: *The "M" in the Model M's name stood for "Monarch," the original maker of the crawler that Allis-Chalmers purchased. The crawler developed up to 30 drawbar horsepower and had four forward gears.*

AULTMAN-TAYLOR

The Aultman & Taylor Machinery Company of Mansfield, Ohio, made some excellent early tractors, known as Aultman-Taylors, starting in 1910, but the firm was absorbed into the Advance-Rumely Thresher Company of LaPorte, Indiana, by the mid-1920s.

BATES

The Bates Tractor Company, like so many gas tractor makers in the days of steam traction engines, fitted cabs to its models before World War I. However, Madison Bates's most memorable tractor was the Steel Mule of 1916 with tracks at the rear and steered wheels at the front.

Bates had worked for the Olds Engine Works, which spawned both the Oldsmobile and REO automobiles, and his Steel Mule looked set to be another major seller. British car and truck maker Herbert Austin obtained European rights before launching his own mass-produced Austin tractors.

In the 1920s, Bates realized his machine was too specialized, so he reverted to straightforward wheeled or crawler machines, the latter produced into the late 1930s.

BULL

The Little Bull tractor was famous as the first of the small, inexpensive gas-powered tractors to be built in quantity.

The Bull Tractor Company of Minneapolis, Minnesota, was founded in 1913 by a group of businessmen, some of whom had previous tractor experience. The Little Bull retailed for $335, resulting in a spate of orders and 4,000 tractors sold in 1914—a production record at the time. Beginning in 1915, engines were made by the associated firm Toro Motors Company, also of Minneapolis and named after the Spanish word for "bull"; the Toro business later spawned a long line of yard tractors. Canada's Massey-Harris aided in selling the Bull.

But the unconventional Little Bull, with its horizontal engine, single driven wheel, and tricycle layout, soon came up against conventional four-wheelers. The arrival of the Fordson in the United States in 1918 and the decision of the Minneapolis Steel & Machinery Company, builder of the Twin City tractor, to cease Bull production assistance spelled a speedy end to the Bull after a promising start.

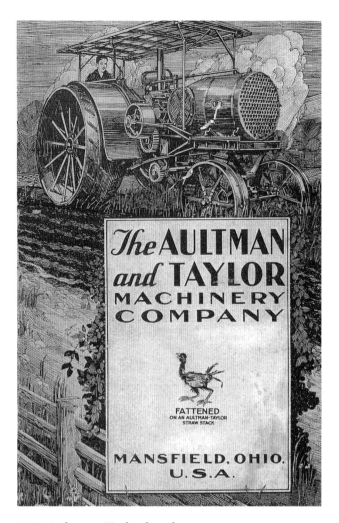

1921 Aultman-Taylor brochure
Aultman-Taylor's famous logo showing a skin-and-bones chicken "fattened on an Aultman-Taylor straw stack," symbolizing the efficiency of the firm's products and the small amount of leftover waste.

CASE

The J. I. Case Threshing Machine Company of Racine, Wisconsin, was known as "the threshing machine king," but the regal firm was also one of the great builders of steam traction engines, starting in 1876 and continuing in production until 1924. As early as 1892, Case experimented with gas-powered tractors, but it was not until twenty years later that the firm's first production gas tractor, the 30/60, was offered, soon followed by more compact models from 1913.

The best-known Case tractors from 1916 were the Crossmotors with their vertical four-cylinder engines placed transversely across the frame. Just when the principal rivals were settling on a conventional layout, and the Wallis tractor had shown the way with a form of unitary frame, Case went in its own direction and built thousands of successful Crossmotors.

In 1929, the Case Models L and C switched to a fore-and-aft engine, but there was still a unique feature in the enclosed chain drive. Because they picked up dirt, chains had fallen out of fashion, but Case buried them in a transmission case and gained the benefit of torque loadings spread over more teeth than with conventional gears, with the added advantage of easier adjustment and replacement.

Between the world wars, Case acquired two respected tractor and implement makers: the Emerson-Brantingham Implement Company of Rockford, Illinois, and the Rock Island Plow Company of Rock Island, Illinois, owner of the rights to the Heider

1900s Case steam tractor brochure
Right: *Case ruled the roost with its steam tractors from their launch in 1876 until 1924, when the famous firm halted steam production and concentrated on gas tractors.*

1919 Case 10/18 Crossmotor
Below: *The 10/18 Crossmotor was a revised version of the original 9/18, which was launched in 1916. The 10/18 had a four-cylinder kerosene engine with a bore and stroke of 3.875x5 inches (96.875x125 mm).*

1930s Rock Island

A Rock Island with Buda 18/35 engine shown in a Canadian agent's brochure of about 1930. Case acquired Rock Island in 1937 and discontinued its tractors.

tractor. In 1935, Case introduced its Motor Lift, a mechanical implement hitch. By the mid-1930s, Case had become the United States's third largest maker of tractors.

Subsequent developments included the adoption of diesel engines in 1953 and the takeover of French tractor producer SFV in the late 1950s. Case was acquired by Tenneco of Houston, Texas, in 1967, and Britain's David Brown joined the group in 1972. The early 1970s saw Case develop its first massive four-wheel-drive machines, an area that the larger makers normally left to specialists like the Steiger Tractor Company of Fargo, North Dakota, which Tenneco also acquired in 1986. In 1985, Tenneco obtained much of International Harvester to create the major new brand of Case International. In 1994, Tenneco separated the Case Corporation into a new company with products identified as Case-IH.

1937 Case CC3

Above: *This 1937 CC3 17/27 horsepower featured Motor Lift, which took the manual strain out of some jobs and allowed mounted instead of trailed implements to be used.*

1938 Case Model C brochure
Right: *The Case Model C was capable of pulling two or three plow bottoms whereas its larger sibling, the Model L, could handle three to five plows. Both tractors featured fore-and-aft valve-in-head engines and internal chain drive.*

1950s Case VA brochure
Case promised "Proved Power in a Smaller Package" with its row-crop VA models.

1948 Case VAH
Left, top: *Only about 2,000 of the special high-clearance VAH model was built between 1947 and 1955, compared with more than 100,000 of the standard VA and VAC 15/22-horsepower models from 1942. Owner: Norm Seveik of Northfield, Minnesota, USA.*

1941 Case DEX
Left, bottom: *The DEX was a special model designed for the 1941 Lend-Lease Act and was based on Model D components. This 1941 DEX was resplendent in the Flambeau Red color scheme adopted by Case a couple of years earlier.*

1950 Case DO
Above: *The "O" in the Case DO's name stood for "Orchard," and this specialized model was fitted with streamlined sheet metal designed to minimize crop damage during orchard work.*

1956 Case Model 300
Right: *The Model 300 row-crop was built from 1956 to 1957, when it became the diesel 301. It was the smallest of the new Flambeau Red and Desert Sand range.*

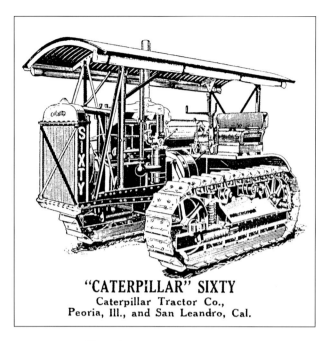

"CATERPILLAR" SIXTY
Caterpillar Tractor Co.,
Peoria, Ill., and San Leandro, Cal.

1925 Caterpillar Sixty
The forerunners of Caterpillar, the Holt Manufacturing Company and both Daniel and Cleo Best's firms, concentrated on building huge tracklayer and wheeled tractors suitable for logging and farming the soft Californian soil. The 60-horsepower Sixty carried on the tradition.

1934 Caterpillar Seventy-Five
Caterpillar was one of the American diesel pioneers, with experiments as early as 1929. This is the gigantic Seventy-Five of 1934 with six-cylinder engine.

CATERPILLAR, HOLT, AND BEST

The 1925 amalgamation of archrival tracklayer tractor firms, the C. L. Best Gas Traction Company of Elmhurst, California, and Holt Manufacturing Company of Stockton, California, created the Caterpillar Tractor Company of Peoria, Illinois. Holt had absorbed the forerunner of the C. L. Best firm, the Daniel Best Company of San Leandro, California, in 1908.

The descriptive "Caterpillar" name had been used on Holt's crawlers since 1904 and came to be a generic term for the whole breed. Many other firms, large and small, made crawlers but Caterpillar became the best-known producer, especially after pioneering work with diesels from 1929 and series diesel production three years later. Gas/kerosene and diesel models were made for agriculture in the 1930s, and then diesel took over as Caterpillar's main power source. A 1970s development was SA diesels in which a solenoid connected to the gearshift gave extra fuelling for maximum output in higher gears. This gave crawlers the speed of the new breed of four-wheel drives and, with recent rubber track developments, kept them competitive for farm work.

From its headquarters in Peoria, Illinois, Caterpillar currently builds farm and construction equipment used around the world. It has factories in England, Scotland, and elsewhere in Europe.

CLETRAC

The Cleveland Tractor Company of Cleveland, Ohio, started building motor plows in 1916. One of the chief stockholders was Rollin White of the White Motor Company of Cleveland, Ohio, which also built trucks, cars, and later tractors. Following its Cleveland Motor Plow, Cletrac soon crafted its own light crawlers, which in their day were almost as well known in farming circles as Caterpillars.

Cletrac was among the first to offer truly compact diesel models in the 1930s, using proprietary Hercules engines. It added wheeled tractors in 1939, but these quickly disappeared when Oliver acquired the business in 1944. Oliver-Cletrac crawlers continued to 1965, bringing Rollin White's brainchild back into the corporate fold of the White Motor Corporation.

Cletracs were exported to Britain, sometimes under the name of local agent Blaw Knox, and in 1937 were the only crawlers with controlled differential steering that gave full use of engine power at all times.

1933 Cletrac brochure
By 1933, Cletrac offered five crawler models ranging from 15 to 83 horsepower.

1934 Caterpillar Seventy-Five
The Caterpillar diesel was started by a small pony, or donkey, engine mounted on the side.

GIANTS *of* POWER *for the* farmer

Cletrac
Crawler Tractors

John Deere

Starting with the renowned plows made by John Deere in the late 1800s, Deere & Company of Moline, Illinois, grew to become one of today's major worldwide agricultural firms.

Deere started limited tractor production before acquiring in 1918 the Waterloo Gasoline Engine Company of Waterloo, Iowa, maker of the successful Waterloo Boy tractor.

The Waterloo Boy gave way to the classic John Deere D of 1923, which was gradually developed until 1953. It had an unusual layout with a horizontal two-cylinder engine lying with the cylinder heads at the front with enclosed-chain final drive. This typified many sizes of "Poppin' Johnnies" or "Johnny Poppers" all the way to 1960, although from 1937 to 1946 there were also the little Models L and LA with vertical Hercules twins.

From 1938, the Deere tractor family look was redesigned with streamlined frontal styling by industrial designer Henry Dreyfuss. An all-new model in 1949 was the R with Deere's first diesel motor. This was John Deere's most powerful tractor to date, developing 34/43 horsepower and featuring a gasoline pony engine for starting.

In the 1950s, live PTO and improved Powr-Trol hydraulics arrived on the 40 to 80 Series, and subsequent 20 Series. The largest tractors boasted six-speed transmissions and power steering.

In 1959, Deere debuted its first big four-wheel drives, and then in 1960, a whole new breed of revolutionary vertical four- and six-cylinder-engined models paved the way for the modern John Deeres. Many of the modern Deeres are made in Germany, where John Deere acquired the famous Lanz factory in 1955.

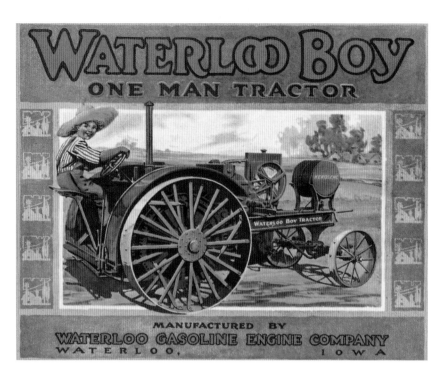

1910s Waterloo Boy brochure
Above: *Deere needed a tractor for its broad list of farm equipment, so in 1918 it purchased the Waterloo Gasoline Engine Company and added the famous Waterloo Boy tractor to its line.*

1930 Deere Model GP
Facing page: *John Deere's GP, or General Purpose, was a 10/20 tractor with one of the first widely available power lifts. The roots of the GP go back to the 1928 introduction of the Model C, which was renamed the GP after only 110 tractors were built. The GP was replaced in 1935 by the Model B.*

1920s Deere Model D brochure
Above: *The Waterloo Boy gave way to the Model D, which made its debut in 1923. The new D firmly established Deere's name and reputation as a tractor manufacturer. The D started as a 15/27 tractor and by the end of its production life had grown to 38/42.*

1930s Deere Models A and B brochure
Above: *Deere's Model A of 1934 and smaller B of 1935 made famous the "Poppin' Johnny" two-cylinder horizontal engine.*

1935 Deere Model B
Left: *The Model B of 1935 was powered by Deere's beloved engine with its two horizontal cylinders set side by side. The B was rated at 9/14 horsepower whereas the larger Model A fathered 18/24 horsepower.*

1930s Deere Model AW

Above: *A wide-front Deere AW parked by a 1930s Ford V-8 coupe in front of the Spencerville, Indiana, covered bridge. Owner: Don Wolf of Indiana, USA.*

1950s Deere Model 50

Right: *The Model 50 was introduced in 1952 and remained in production until 1956. In 1954, it became the first mass-produced tractor with power steering.*

1940s Deere Model H
Above: *Available from 1939 to 1947, John Deere's Model H was a 12-horse-power machine suitable for row-crop work with mid- and rear-mounted implements. Owner: Kenneth Anderson of the USA.*

1960 John Deere 435
Left: *The 1960 season marked the end of the much-loved side-by-side Deere twins, and the new Deere 435 was powered by a GM Detroit two-stroke diesel. At the same time, Deere also launched its own four- and six-cylinder diesels. As the decal proclaimed, the 435 had power steering. Owner: Don Wolf of Indiana, USA.*

FORDSON AND FORD

Henry Ford was a farmer's son. From the earliest days of his successful car firm, Ford was looking at ways of easing the farmer's burden—and of course benefiting his own business. After many experiments with tractor designs, Ford shipped his first Fordson to Great Britain in 1917 and entered the North America market in 1918. The Fordson had a similar engine to the Ford Model T car, which kept costs to a minimum and allowed a sale price as low as $395 in 1922. Its revolutionary cast-iron unit frame incorporated the sump, transmission case, and front axle and radiator supports.

From these humble beginnings, Ford became the largest American tractor producer in 1918, when 30,000 Fordsons were built. The Fordson also won fame in Britain for helping to alleviate famine during World War I.

Ford opened a factory in Cork, Ireland, and tractors were made sporadically there from 1919 to the opening of the Dagenham plant outside London in the early 1930s. American production ceased in 1928, after an amazing 738,000 Fordsons had been sold. From 1928, Ford imported English-built Fordsons back into the United States and Canada.

The original Fordson Model F evolved into the similar-looking N in 1929 with larger cylinder bores to increase power to 27 horsepower, and this Standard Model continued with various improvements until the end of World War II.

Meanwhile in the United States, Ford began to produce the Ford 9N tractor in 1939, incorporating Irishman Harry Ferguson's brilliant hydraulic three-point hitch and draft control. After the war and Henry Ford's death, the Ford company and Ferguson fell out, leading to a prolonged lawsuit over Ford's alleged patent infringements that resulted in a massive settlement in favor of Ferguson. Ford continued to build its renowned N Series tractors while Ferguson began production of his own models.

In Britain, the Fordson E27N Major was built for world markets, and in the United States, a range of five models in 1955 put the firm into just about every popular horsepower range. Ford had also bought implement maker Wood Bros., Inc., to offer its own line of implements.

In 1961, Ford released its biggest tractor yet, the six-cylinder 60-drawbar-horsepower 6000, followed by the 8000 in 1968, and the turbocharged 9000 in 1969, which produced 130 horsepower.

In 1986, Ford acquired the Sperry New Holland Company of New Holland, Pennsylvania, and in 1987, purchased Canada's Versatile. In 1993, Fiat of Italy bought the Ford tractor name, and under its control, New Holland continues to build New Holland Ford tractors for farms around the globe.

1930 Fordson advertisement

Gentleman's Agreement, 1938
Harry Ferguson, left, and Henry Ford meet in 1938 following Ferguson's demonstration to shake hands on a plan to join forces in building what would become the revolutionary Ford-Ferguson 9N.

1946 Ford-Ferguson 2N

Above: *The 2N enjoyed a six-year production run. Even though the first and last years were only partial years, almost 200,000 were made, more than twice the number of 9Ns. This 2N has a Sherman Step-Up transmission giving six forward and two reverse speeds. Headlights and grill guard were options when this 1946 2N was new. Owner: Floyd Dominique of Napoleon, Ohio, USA.*

1940 Ford-Ferguson 9N

Left: *The 9N was introduced in 1939, hence its model nomenclature. It was powered by a 119.7-ci (1,960-cc) inline four-cylinder with bore and stroke of 3.187x3.75 inches (79.6x93.75 mm). "It was a bad day for old Dobbin," noted one newspaper's announcement of the new tractor, as the 9N was targeted to replace horse teams on farms.*

1948 Ford 8N

Above: *Despite Harry Ferguson's lawsuits, the 8N was produced from late 1947 to 1952. To battle the Ford tractor, Ferguson began producing his TE-20 model. This 8N is better than new after being completely remanufactured by N-Complete, the Ford N Series specialist in Wilkinson, Indiana, USA.*

1949 Ford 8N

Left: *Following the break from Harry Ferguson, Ford launched its new 8N tractor in 1947. The new model was a thinly disguised update of the 2N, and Ferguson contested several of its features in a drawn-out court battle. Owner: Floyd Dominique of Napoleon, Ohio, USA.*

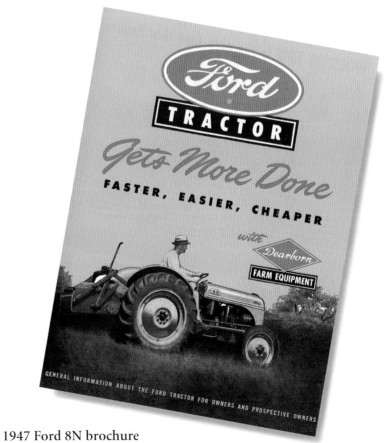

1947 Ford 8N brochure

1960 Ford 601 Workmaster

Above: *The 601 Workmaster debuted in 1957 as an updated version of 1955's 600. The 601 was powered by a 134-ci (2,195-cc) engine, while the Powermaster series of tractors featured 172-ci (2,817-cc) engines. Owner: Mike Hanna of Pendleton, Indiana, USA.*

1953 Ford NAA Golden Jubilee

Right: *The Ford Motor Company celebrated its fiftieth anniversary in 1953 with new car, truck, and tractor models. The new Ford NAA tractor had a round medallion on its nose incorporating a new tractor logo: a corn stalk in the center of a shield topped by the Ford script-in-oval and the words, "Golden Jubilee Model 1903–1953." The 1953 Jubilee can be distinguished from the 1954 and later Model 600s by the nose medallion. Only the '53s had the Golden Jubilee words. Owner: Floyd Dominique of Napoleon, Ohio, USA.*

1961 Ford 971 LPG Workmaster

Facing page: *The 971 was available powered by either gas-fueled or liquefied petroleum gas (LPG) engines. In 1959, the Ford Workmaster series reverted to the red-and-gray paint scheme, paying homage to the great 8N tractor of late 1947 to 1952. Owner: Dwight Emstrom of the USA.*

HART-PARR

Starting in 1897 as engine builders, Charles Hart and Charles Parr made their first tractor in Charles City, Iowa, in 1901. This is generally credited with being the first successful production tractor, and a few years later, the Hart-Parr Company's sales manager was said to have first coined the now-universal term "tractor."

Hart-Parr specialized in massive oil-cooled gas tractors in direct competition with the steamers usually used for heavy haulage and breaking the prairies. In 1918, following the unsuccessful Little Red Devil, Hart-Parr introduced smaller, more conventional machines with cross-mounted motors similar to the subsequent Case. Hart-Parr's lightweight Crossmotors were built in several sizes and became popular.

In 1929, Hart-Parr merged with five firms, including the Oliver Chilled Plow Company of South Bend, Indiana, and the tractor maker Nichols & Shepard Company of Battle Creek, Michigan, to create the Oliver Farm Equipment Corporation of Chicago, Illinois. Rebadged as Oliver Hart-Parr tractors, Hart-Parr models remained in the line for several years.

1926 Hart-Parr 12/24 Model E
Hart-Parr was one of the key constituents in the merger of 1929 that formed the Oliver Farm Equipment Corporation. This is an example of the type of tractor it was making in 1926, the twin-cylinder 12/24-horsepower Model E.

HUBER

The Huber Manufacturing Company of Marion, Ohio, made some of the first gas-powered production tractors. Debuting in 1898, the tractor designs were based on Benjamin Vanduzen's patents. Huber continued building tractors until World War II, when the firm switched to construction machinery. In 1950, Huber made the Global tractor for a separate marketing company to sell.

1920s Huber Super Four advertisement
Huber's Super Four debuted in 1921 with a Midwest engine providing 15/30 horsepower.

1911 International Titan Type D

The massive International Titan Type D first appeared in 1910 with two gigantic side-by-side 9x14-inch (225x350-mm) cylinders that fired simultaneously, producing about 45 horsepower.

INTERNATIONAL HARVESTER

The International Harvester Company of Chicago, Illinois, was formed in 1902 with capital of $120 million from the merger of the rival McCormick Harvesting Machine Company and Deering Harvester Company, both of Chicago, Illinois, and several other firms. In 1906, International built 25 15-horsepower tractors, followed by 200 more in 1907. By 1965, the 4,000,000th IH tractor was produced.

International's early machines became known as Moguls and Titans, and tended to be massive. Smaller versions were available from around 1910, and thousands of these were exported to Europe during World War I. They were archaic-looking even by the standards of the time and were superseded by the enclosed 8/16 Juniors in 1917 with their firewall-mounted radiators.

Unit-frame McCormick-Deering 15/30 models with front-mounted radiators followed in 1921; two years later came the 10/20 with advanced overhead-valve four-cylinder engines with ball-bearing-mounted crankshafts. The 10/20 was one of the first popular tractors available with a PTO. These tractors were better engineered, better equipped, yet more expensive rivals to the ubiquitous Fordson. The 10/20 in particular proved to be immensely popular with 215,000 sold up to the start of World War II.

International was truly international. The firm built a factory in Hamilton, Ontario, Canada, followed by its first European plant at Norrkköpping, Sweden, in 1905. Other plants in Germany, France, and Russia followed.

The lightweight general-purpose Farmall arrived in 1924 and was available with a wide range of mounted implements. After a slow start, the Farmall became a great success, revolutionizing the role of the tractor in agriculture. The 100,000th Farmall was produced in 1930.

Caterpillar had already proved the fuel economy benefits of diesels when International became the first in the United States to offer a diesel-powered wheeled tractor, the WD-40 of 1934.

International also made TracTracTor crawlers, and joined its rivals in the trend to streamlined styling in the later 1930s. The little Farmall A of 1939 with its offset engine to give Culti-Vision for mid- and front-mounted implements resembled the Allis-Chalmers B and opened up yet another field of opportunities.

World War II and the postwar years saw a massive expansion of International model types and the addition of new factories in Britain, France, Germany, Australia, and elsewhere. Giant four-wheel drives came in the mid-1960s.

International bought a share of the Steiger Tractor Company of Fargo, North Dakota, before Tenneco of Houston, Texas, acquired International in 1984. The tractor range was then incorporated into Tenneco's Case subsidiary to create Case International. The Case Corporation currently has several plants in the United States and Canada, while its principal European site is at the former International factory in Doncaster, England.

1918 International 8/16
Below, top: *International's 8/16 was an important forerunner of the famous Farmall as it proved there was a market for a lightweight tractor. It was introduced in 1917 and built until 1922.*

1930 Farmall Regular
Below, bottom: *The Regular was such an ingenious concept that it changed little from its introduction in 1924 through the end of production in 1932, when it was replaced by the F-20. A 1947 International KB-6 truck stands in the background. Owner: Larry Kinsey of Indiana, USA.*

1930 McCormick-Deering 10/20

Left, top: *International's McCormick-Deering 10/20 was an immensely popular standard tractor with great sales even during the reign of the Farmall. Some 215,000 examples were built from 1923 to 1939, with the peak coming in 1929, when almost 40,000 were sold. The 10/20 had a four-cylinder, valve-in-head kerosene engine with a bore and stroke of 4.25x5 inches (106.25x125 mm), displacing 284 ci (4.7 liters). Owner: Larry Kinsey of Indiana, USA.*

1930 Farmall Regular

Left, bottom: *The Farmall Regular was powered by a four-cylinder, valve-in-head engine with a bore and stroke of 3.75x5 inches (93.75x125 mm).*

1930 Farmall Regular

Below: *Business end of the well-restored Farmall Regular. Owner: Larry Kinsey of Indiana, USA.*

1950 Farmall H
A Farmall H tricycle row-crop of 1950 with an Allis-Chalmers in the background at Lampson's Cedar View Orchard in Iowa.

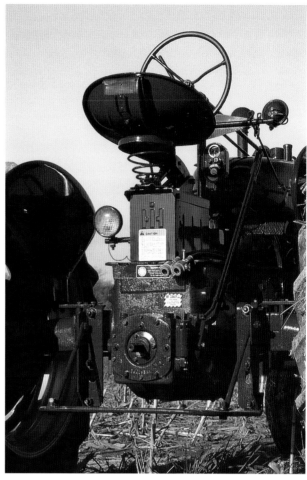

1954 Farmall Super MD-TA
Above: *The MD-TA had a PTO but did not have a hydraulic implement lift. This model featured five forward gears.*

1954 Farmall Super MD-TA
Below: *The MD-TA was a diesel version of the famous M with lever-controlled Torque Amplifier. Restored by its owner Donald Schaeffer, this Super MD-TA sets out on a cold spring morning.*

MINNEAPOLIS-MOLINE

A merger of far-reaching consequences saw the makers of the successful Twin City, Minneapolis, and Universal tractors join forces in 1929 to establish a new, full line of agricultural implements as the Minneapolis-Moline Company of Minneapolis, Minnesota. Twin City tractors had been built by the Minneapolis Steel & Machinery Company of Minneapolis; Minneapolis tractors had come from the Minneapolis Threshing Machine Company of Hopkins, Minnesota; and Universal motor cultivators had been made by the Moline Plow Company of Moline, Illinois.

Minneapolis Steel & Machinery had built designs for Case and Bull, as well as its own MS&M machines in the 1910s. These tended to be prairie monsters with drum-type horizontal radiators. However, a lighter model made for the Grain Growers Co-op in Canada in 1914 developed into the range of excellent Twin City models, some of which lasted to the creation of Minneapolis-Moline, such as the 17/28. The 1919 12/20 was probably the first tractor with four valves per cylinder—a feature shared with the contemporary Bugatti sports car.

The subsequent Minneapolis-Moline tractors went through many of the same evolutionary stages as their other big rivals and, in 1935, were the first to fit high-compression gas motors to take advantage of higher-grade leaded fuel. A full cab with heater and wipers was an industry first on the UDLX "Comfortractor" of 1938, the same year that streamlined "Visionlined" styling was adopted, along with another advance: five forward gears.

Minneapolis-Molines were popular Lend-Lease tractors during World War II, but the competitive field in the 1950s shook the farming giant. In 1963, Minneapolis-Moline joined the White Motor Corporation's empire. The famous combination of names was finally phased out in the mid-1970s.

NICHOLS & SHEPARD

Before starting the Aultman-Taylor firm, Henry Taylor worked for the respected Nichols & Shepard Company, a famous maker of threshing machines in Battle Creek, Michigan. Nichols & Shepard added steam traction engines, and then, in 1911, its Oil-Gas tractor. This firm and its tractors lasted until the 1929 merger with Oliver.

1918 Twin City 16/30
The 16/30 came from a range of advanced 12- to 60-horsepower tractors offered by the Minneapolis Steel & Machinery Company in 1918. This model was powered by a four-cylinder engine with a 5x7.5-inch (125x187.5-mm) bore and stroke. Owner: Sue Dougan of Iowa, USA.

1918 Moline Universal Model D
The Moline Plow Company's Model D 9/18-horsepower motor plow was introduced in 1918 and remained in production until 1923. This Universal boasted electric starting, a four-cylinder engine, and a curious back-to-front radiator fan that was fortunately well cowled. Owner: Sue Dougan of Iowa, USA.

1935 Minneapolis-Moline MTA Universal

Above: *The Twin City tractor was one of the constituents of the new Minneapolis-Moline grouping of 1929. It lived on for a while in various models, including this MTA Universal row-crop machine. Owner: Roger Mohr of Vail, Iowa, USA.*

1939 Minneapolis-Moline Z brochure

Left: *The Visionlined Z was powered by a 186-ci (3.1-liter) four-cylinder engine rated at 16/23 horsepower.*

1944 Minneapolis-Moline R
Above, top: *The R was the smallest in the Minneapolis-Moline's range of the era.*

1944 Minneapolis-Moline R
Above, bottom: *This Minne-Mo Model R was factory fitted with a steel cab and mid-mounted implements. Owner: Roger Mohr of Vail, Iowa, USA.*

Minneapolis-Moline UDLX
Right: *The UDLX Comfortractor featured Minneapolis-Moline's luxury cab.*

1930s Oliver 90 brochure
The famous Oliver 90 was built from 1937 until 1953. The 90 featured a valve-in-head engine with a 4.75x6.25-inch (118.85x156.25-mm) bore and stroke.

OLIVER

The Oliver Farm Equipment Corporation of Chicago, Illinois, was the result of another merger in the farm implement business that saw the Oliver Chilled Plow Company of South Bend, Indiana, joining forces with the Hart-Parr Company of Charles City, Iowa, and others.

The new firm's tractors were initially called Oliver Hart-Parr, and were impressive machines built to a high standard. Oliver tractors were streamlined in the mid-1930s, and six-cylinder models became a specialty.

The name Oliver carried on for a few years after the 1960 takeover by the White Motor Corporation. During the 1960s, some models were produced for Oliver by Britain's David Brown, and Italy's Fiat and SAME.

1936 Oliver Hart-Parr 70 and 1948 Oliver 77
Above: *Two generations of well-loved Oliver tractors. In the foreground is a 1936 Oliver Hart-Parr 70 Row-Crop with a 1948 Oliver 77 Fleetline Standard parked in front of the machine shed. The streamlined 77 was the replacement for the venerable 70, whose lineage stretched back to Hart-Parr days.*

1939 Oliver 70 brochure
Right: *Oliver's 70 was available in the tricycle row-crop format shown on the cover of this brochure as well as in standard and orchard configurations.*

1950s Oliver 70 Orchard brochure

Above: *Contemporary with the angular-looking 90, Oliver made the streamlined 70 with a six-cylinder engine. This is the faired orchard model.*

1952 Oliver HG

Right: *Oliver's HG crawler was a continuation of the Cletrac tracklayer lineage, which had been bought by Oliver in 1944. The HG had controlled differential steering that gave full-power turns.*

1958 Oliver Super 99

Above: *Oliver's Super 99 was a true hot rod. It was powered by a three-cylinder, two-stroke, supercharged GM Detroit diesel displacing 213 ci (3.5 liters). The Roots-type blower forced in more mixture and helped the engine develop 73/78 horsepower at 1,675 rpm. Owner: Dick Ramminger of Wisconsin, USA.*

1952 Oliver HG

Left: *The Oliver HG was rated at 18/22 horsepower as a two-plow machine with three forward gears and one reverse.*

Samson

Another once-familiar name was the Samson Tractor Works of Stockton, California, which made popular low-slung tractors with open straked wheels in World War I. Samson was purchased by General Motors of Pontiac, Michigan, in 1918, as an entry into the tractor market to compete against Henry Ford.

General Motors had high hopes for Samson's Sieve Grip tractor, but quickly realized it was no match for the Fordson. A conventional Model M then competed head on with Ford but lost the battle when GM squandered its advantage on a brief craze for motor cultivators.

1919 Samson Sieve Grip

Surrounded by a circus troupe of midgets, clowns, Gypsies, and monkeys, this ten-year-old Samson Sieve Grip starred on a film set in 1929. Announced in 1914, the Sieve Grip was available as either a 6/12 or 10/25. The firm's colorful motto was "The Strength of Samson in Every Part."

STEIGER

Four-wheel drive had been tried by many tractor makers, although they were usually underfunded inventors or promoters, and the attempts did not last long. Canada's Massey-Harris had made its successful General Purpose four-wheel-drive lightweight in the 1930s. But it was not until the big proprietary-engined tractors of the 1960s that the four-wheel drive idea hit the big time, and by the 1970s, every maker's lineup had to have a big four-wheel drive at the top, often made for the firm in question by the Steiger Tractor Company of Fargo, North Dakota.

The Steiger business stemmed from farming brothers Douglass and Maurice Steiger, who built their own machines from Euclid earthmover parts, starting in 1957. Steiger was acquired by Tenneco in 1986.

MRS of Flora, Mississippi, made similar four-wheel-drive tractors during the same era.

WALLIS

The Wallis Tractor Company of Racine, Wisconsin, pioneered unit construction in tractors. H. M. Wallis was president of the J. I. Case Plow Works, also of Racine but a separate firm from the J. I. Case Threshing Machine Company; he was also president of the Wallis company that made a massive tractor called the Bear in 1902.

Wallis engineers Clarence Eason and Robert Hendrickson patented their one-piece curved boiler-plate frame for the Wallis Cub in 1913. The Cub had an exposed ring-gear drive, but two years later they came up with an improved model in which the enclosed drive ran in oil. The advantages of a one-piece frame, as Henry Ford also realized, was in material savings and in the permanent alignment of all shafts and bearings in the engine and transmission. The Wallis tractor was popular in the 1920s and became the basis for the subsequent Massey-Harris tractor after Canada's Massey bought out Wallis in 1928.

The Wallis was also built briefly in Britain by steam engineers Ruston & Hornsby of Lincoln, England, who had diversified by building internal-combustion-engined gun tractors and then cars.

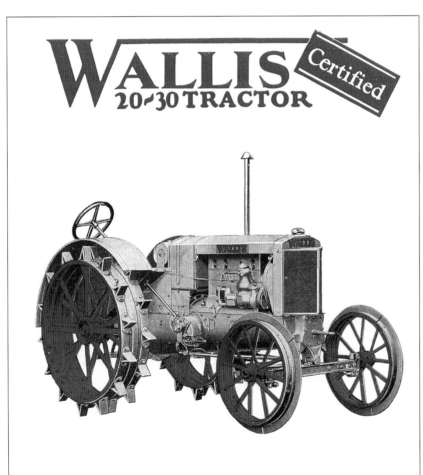

MASSEY-HARRIS CO., Ltd.
ESTABLISHED 1847

Head Office—Toronto, Canada
European Branches—London, Paris, Berlin
Australian Branches—Melbourne, Sydney, Brisbane, Perth, Adelaide

New Zealand Branches—Christchurch, Dunedin, Auckland, Wellington
South American Branches—Buenos Aires, Rosario, Bahia Blanca
South African Branches—Durban, Natal

1928 Wallis 20/30 brochure
The unit-frame Wallis joined the Massey-Harris lineup in 1928. The Wallis's valve-in-head engine delivered 20/30 horsepower.

WATERLOO BOY

The Waterloo Boy tractor was the machine that gave Deere & Company its successful introduction to the tractor business, in 1918. However, the roots of the Waterloo Boy go back much further.

The engineer of the Waterloo Boy was John Froehlich, who in 1892 built a machine that was possibly the world's first internal-combustion-engined tractor, which featured both forward and reverse gears. Froehlich went on to form the Waterloo Gasoline Traction Engine Company of Waterloo, Iowa, but left when fellow directors put resources into engines rather than tractors.

Eventually, in 1912, the successor firm, the Waterloo Gasoline Engine Company, launched the Waterloo Boy. This was a simple, straightforward design, which was imported into Great Britain as the Overtime. More than 8,000 Waterloo Boys had been sold by the time that Deere & Company acquired the firm and its famous tractor in 1918.

WHITE

Although the White Motor Corporation of Cleveland, Ohio, appeared late on the tractor scene, it was an old, established business. White sewing machines were first made in 1866, followed by bicycles, roller skates, machine tools, and steam cars. Then came gas-powered cars and trucks, the latter becoming White's most famous ware. The White truck division was taken over by Sweden's Volvo in 1981.

In 1960, White acquired Oliver. Ironically, Oliver owned Cletrac, which had been established by Rollin White of the same White family origins. Other tractor and implement firms involved with White were Canada's Cockshutt, acquired in 1962, and Minneapolis-Moline, added in 1963. From all these acquisitions, the White Farm Equipment Company of Oak Brook, Illinois, was created in 1973, a division of the White Motor Corporation.

At the start, the White name had simply been added to existing Oliver and Minneapolis-Moline models from 1969, but a big four-wheel drive originally offered by M-M that year could be bought as the White Plainsman in 1970. From this grew the 4-150 available purely as a White Field Boss in 1974. In the

following year, two-wheel-drive Whites with similar styling appeared.

In late 1980, WFE, as White Farm Equipment had become known, was acquired by the TIC Investment Corporation of Dallas, Texas, to start a separate existence independent of White's truck-making past. As part of the AGCO stable in the 1990s, its machines continue as Whites, although its largest four-wheel drives are now known as AGCOSTARS.

1920 Waterloo Boy Model N
Above: *The Waterloo Boy was adopted by John Deere and became the famous firm's first mass-produced tractor. A Ford Model T pickup truck waits in the background. Owner: Don Wolf of Indiana, USA.*

1920 Waterloo Boy Model N
Right: *In 1920, the Model N Waterloo Boy became the first tractor to be tested by the University of Nebraska. It recorded 12 drawbar and 25.5 belt horsepower. Owner: Don Wolf of Indiana, USA.*

TRACTORS *of* OTHER LANDS

⌐◦≫⊶≪◦⌐

Almost every industrialized country has been home to manufacturers of farm tractors at some stage. Unless the country's market was large, prosperous, or protected by tariffs, however, few tractor makers were able to survive the arrival of the multi national builders with their vast development budgets and dealer backup.

1957 Valmet 33D
Facing page: *Finland's principal tractor maker has long been Valmet. This is one of its 1957 Model 33D diesels, which, as the model number implied, developed 33 horsepower.*

1950s Russian XT3-7 brochure
Above: *A 1950s example of a Russian tractor with a 12-horsepower engine, five forward and four reverse gears, and a driving position and lighting that could be swung around for operation in either forward or reverse direction.*

AUSTRIA: LINDNER AND STEYR

Austria is home to Lindner and Steyr tractors. Lindner made compact tractors starting in 1947, before graduating to mid-horsepower models in the 1970s.

Like Zetor of Czechoslovakia, Steyr achieved early success making guns; Steyr's logo features a circular badge representing a target. Steyr made bicycles before expanding its line in 1920 by adding cars as well as Excelsior motor plows, which were built under license from Laurin & Klement of Czechoslovakia. Steyr then offered trucks and, starting in 1928, farm tractors.

Steyr's tractors were initially inspired by the Fordson. The firm built a few early models before beginning mass production of tractors in 1947. Steyrs were powered primarily by single-cylinder engines of under 20 horsepower, although twins were also offered. In the first eighteen years, Steyr sold a remarkable 160,000 tractors.

Starting in the 1950s, Steyr made tractors with increasingly more horsepower; it offered a full range of models beginning in the 1970s. Its tractor business, latterly using MWM and Perkins engines, was bought by Tenneco of Houston, Texas, in 1996. Tenneco is also the owner of Case International, and some Steyr models were integrated into the Case IH range.

BRAZIL: MALVES

Malves of São Paolo is one of the few indigenous South American tractor manufacturers. Most of the other South American makers are derivatives of North American or European tractors, but the Malves tractors of the 1980s were locally designed. Malves engines, however, were based on Daimler-Benz and Cummins powerplants.

CHINA

Like the Soviet Union, China has numerous tractor manufacturers, although most of the Chinese tractors tend to be of 1950s or more recent origin.

1960 Steyr 188 brochure
Above: *Steyr's 188 tractor was powered by a two-cylinder, water-cooled diesel that delivered 27 horsepower.*

1970s Malves MD 700 brochure
Below: *Malves's 70-horsepower MD 700 had a 191-ci (3.10-liter), four-cylinder diesel and ten forward gears.*

CZECHOSLOVAKIA: LAURIN & KLEMENT, SKODA, PRAGA, AND ZETOR

Czechoslovakia has been home to several prolific tractor manufacturers. Laurin & Klement made its Excelsior motor plows starting in 1911.

Emil Skoda acquired an engineering business in 1869, and from the mid-1920s up to World War II, Skoda made general-purpose tractors. In 1925, Skoda bought Laurin & Klement.

Like the Hungarian RABA, Liaz introduced large four-wheel-drive machines in the 1970s. Liaz was associated with Skoda.

Praga of Prague was founded in 1871. It made cars from 1907 and built general-purpose tractors from the mid-1920s up to World War II.

The other great Czech name is Zetor of Brno, which grew in 1945 from a business that manufactured aircraft, ball-bearings, and guns; in keeping with its wares, the firm's logo featured a rifled barrel. In 1947, Zetor exported 1,000 tractors. By the early 1950s, the firm was building 10,000 machines per year, and 20,000 ten years later.

1960s Zetor Diesel 3045

Zetor featured disengageable four-wheel drive on the larger models in its Unified series. This mid-1960s Diesel 3045 was one of the last of the "old shape" Zetor models. With four-wheel drive and 50 horsepower, the tractor sold at a competitive price in the West. Owner: Paul Hembury.

East Germany: ZT

Of similar appearance to the Czech Zetor Crystal, East Germany's ZT tractor of the 1970s was built by Schönebeck and powered by a license-built MAN engine. Sold abroad as the Fortschritt, it was descended from the various German tractor makers that had ended up in the East after the post–World War II partition; these included FAMO, Horch, and the old Normag works that became Nordhausen.

Finland: Valmet

Valmet was a classic example of turning swords to plowshares when the Finnish state armaments firm introduced a tractor in 1949. After a slow start, the 3,000th Valmet was built in early 1955, and the 330,000th in 1989.

The first Valmets were powered by a single-cylinder 12-horsepower engine, followed by a 92-ci (1.5-liter) four-cylinder in 1953, and a 165-ci (2.7-liter) three-cylinder diesel in 1957 for the 33D model with 37 brake horsepower.

Brazil bought 1,000 Valmets in 1960, and Valmet established a factory in Brazil in 1962, making tractors with license-built MWM engines. The 20,000th Brazilian Valmet rolled off the assembly line in June 1971, followed by the 100,000th in 1978. The Brazilian firm gained market leadership in the 100-plus horsepower market and made a success of alcohol-fuelled engines.

In 1964, Valmet's new 565 model arrived with a synchronized gearbox of Case origin featuring six forward and two reverse gears. At the same time, forest tractors became available and built-in safety cabs were standardized. Turbocharging arrived in 1969, by which time some models had hydrostatic crawler gears.

Valmet and Sweden's Volvo pooled their tractor resources in 1979, and in 1980, exhaust pressure wave supercharging was tried in the Valmet Comprex model. Valmet tractors also began to be assembled in 1980 in Portugal and in the Scania truck factory in Tanzania.

In 1985, Valmet and Volvo parted ways when Valmet bought out Volvo's 50 percent interest in their joint Scantrac Nordic venture. By 1996, the Valmet tractor business was jointly owned with the Finnish government and Partek, makers of Hiab truck loaders. In the late 1990s, Valmet was supplying engines to the largest French-built Massey-Fergusons and to AGCO's Danish-built combines; in return, it was receiving M-F chassis and transmissions for its own high-horsepower models.

1955 Valmet 20 brochure
Left: *Valmet's Model 20 had a four-cylinder engine developing up to 23 horsepower on gasoline but featured only three forward gears.*

1957 Valmet 33D
Above: *The 33 was a newcomer in 1956, entering Valmet's model line alongside the existing gas/kerosene 20-horsepower and original 15-horsepower models that were developed in 1949 and entered production in 1953. The three-cylinder 33D continued to 1959, when the model developed into the 359D. Like Steyr, Zetor, Vickers, and many other armament makers, Valmet saw tractors as a replacement for the guns it had been producing. Owner: Sam Read.*

1950s GeDe 20 Diesel brochure
Above: *Among a small number of Dutch makers was GeDe, which was short for Geurtsen of Deventer. The GeDe 20 was powered by a two-cylinder, air-cooled Deutz diesel from Germany that delivered 18/22 horsepower.*

HUNGARY: HSCS, DUTRA, AND RABA

The Hofherr-Schrantz-Clayton-Shuttleworth Company (HSCS) was formed in Budapest in 1900 as a collaboration between Hungarian interests and the famous Clayton & Shuttleworth Company of England, which had become a big name in Central Europe with its steam plows. HSCS's local factories were bought by Hungarian interests in 1912, and the firm made hot-bulb tractors from the 1930s to the 1950s. HSCS became Dutra of Budapest and began building four-wheel-drive tractors in 1961 under the Dutra name.

The former RABA railroad workshops at Gyor acquired a license to make American Steiger tractors in the 1970s. In 1973, RABA merged with Dutra.

JAPAN: KUBOTA, HINOMOTO, ISEKI, AND KOMATSU

Japan's tractor industry is too modern to have contributed much to the list of classic tractors. However, worthy of note are the miniature Kubotas made since 1960, as well as the Hinomotos, and the small- and medium-horsepower models made by Iseki, which has supplied models to the American White firm since about 1980.

Komatsu made its first crawlers in the 1930s and diesels from 1947. In 1961, Komatsu was granted a license to make Cummins engines in Japan, and since then it has become one of the three largest makers of crawlers in the world. It acquired the remnants of the German Hanomag tractor business in 1989, and this now makes construction machinery, including loaders.

1937 HSCS
This style of 40-horsepower, hot-bulb HSCS tractor was widely used in Europe, Australia, and elsewhere around the globe.

The Netherlands: GeDe

One of the small number of Dutch makers was GeDe, which was short for Geurtsen of Deventer. GeDe produced a variety of tractors following World War II.

Poland: Ursus

Ursus of Warsaw used Czech Zetor components to build its own tractors in the 1950s. In 1978, Ursus was modernized in a massive deal involving Massey-Ferguson and Perkins. Ursus supplied niche models to the 1990s M-F lineup, and at the time of publication, AGCO was alleged to be buying Ursus.

1958 Ursus
The hot-bulb, single-cylinder Ursus was based on the German Lanz Bulldog, although it later became a close relation to the Czech Zetor.

1954 Ursus C45
The "ZMU" badge on the front of this restored 45-horsepower C45 Ursus denoted the tractor maker Zakladow Mechanicznych Ursus of Czeckowice, Warsaw, which had made trucks in the 1920s and 1930s.

ROMANIA: UTB

Uzina Tractorul Brasov (UTB), or "Universal," of Brasov built Fiat tractors under license for Romanian farmers. The Crystal tractor series of 1969 was a joint venture between Universal, which made its driven front axles, and Ursus of Poland, which supplied transmissions.

SOVIET UNION: POUTILOVET, BELARUS, AND TRACTOROEXPORT

The former Soviet Union produced vast numbers of different tractor models since the 1910s. The early tractors were primitive, but they soon gave way to Western technology when in October 1924 the Fordson Model F entered production in Kirov as the Poutilovets tractor. Some 50,000 Poutilovets were made up to April 1932.

In 1930, the vast Volgograd tractor works opened, and in 1931, another tractor factory at Kharkov started producing indigenous machines incorporating American ideas. Many more tractor factories followed, including a works in Vladimir in 1944 and Minsk in 1950, the year in which the first of the Belarus tractors appeared.

Tractoroexport began exporting Soviet tractors around the world in 1961. By the mid-1970s, 250,000 tractors with ratings from 25 to 310 horsepower had been sold—usually at subsidized prices well below that of the capitalist competition. In addition, Vladimir T-25 models were being made in Mexico as Sidenas tractors.

In 1940, the Soviet Union built a total of 20,300 tractors; at the dawn of the 1970s, 550,000 tractors were being produced in the USSR each year, and the Volgograd works alone was making 80,000 DT crawlers annually. By 1972, 1,000,000 Soviet tractors had been built, making the USSR the world's largest maker of tractors.

1970s Universal S445
A late 1970s Universal S445 crawler displaying its Fiat origins.

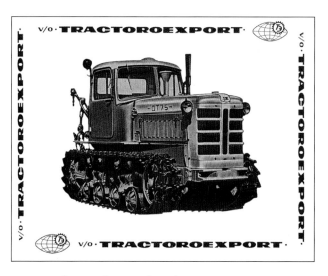

1960s Volgograd DT75 brochure
Volgograd's DT-75 crawler of 1963–1967 featured military-type sprung idlers and a 75-horsepower diesel started by a 10-horsepower pony engine. The Volgograd had full hydraulics.

Spain: Ebro

Ebro of Barcelona assembled Ford cars and trucks in the 1920s and 1930s. It made Ford tractors in the 1950s and 1960s, and in a link with Perkins in 1966, also made Massey-Fergusons. Ebro's own pale-blue models with red wheels evolved from the Massey-Fergusons. In 1975, Ebro acquired the SEMA-Renault tractor factory. Under Japanese Nissan control in the 1980s, Ebro briefly made Kubota tractors of up to 75 horsepower.

Several multinational tractor makers have established factories in Spain through the years.

1970 Ebro 55
Left: *The Fordson Major was made in Spain by Ebro as the Model 55 in 1970.*

1950s Kirovets KD-35 brochure
Below: *From the home of the Russian Fordsons, this was the Kirovets KD-35, made 1947 to 1958.*

SWITZERLAND: BÜHRER, HÜRLIMANN, MEILI, AND VEVEY

Switzerland has been home to several makers of low-profile four-wheel-drive mountain tractors. Surprisingly, this small country also managed to support several producers of full-size conventional tractors.

Bührer of Hinwil, Zürich, began building self-propelled mowers in 1929, added tractors in the 1930s (some with cabs from 1938), and then made diesel models starting in 1941. Three-range gearboxes were an unusual feature beginning in 1954; this was refined ten years later as the fifteen-ratio, shift-on-the-move Tractospeed. Bührer used its own 264-ci (4.33-liter) four-cylinder diesels as well as imported engines, including six-cylinder gasoline Chevrolets. Bührer made the last of a total of 22,600 tractors in 1978.

The other major Swiss name is Hürlimann of Wil, St. Gallen, which also dates to 1929. In 1939, the firm built what it claimed to be the world's first four-cylinder direct-injection diesel-engined tractor. In 1966, Hürlimann was among the first makers to build large-horsepower models, launching a 155-horsepower tractor powered by Hürlimann's own six-cylinder engine. Since then, Hürlimann bought many Italian SAME components and was later acquired by the firm. The current Hürlimann models are of Italian origin.

Last but not least are Meili of Schaffhausen and Vevey of Vevey, near Montreux, which both made large tractors in the 1950s. Meili continues to build compact mountain types.

Vevey's first tractor of 1936 had five forward gears and CLM opposed-piston two-stroke or more conventional four-stroke Saurer diesels. After World War II, Buda-Lanova engines were used in Vevey tractors with ingenious PTOs for mid-mounted implements. Thus, rotary cultivators on the offside could till the ground that had been turned by the previous pass of the plow at the same time that more furrows were being turned at the rear. Veveys frequently featured sprung front axles and latterly had Perkins diesels. Vevey gave up tractors in 1962 in favor of turbines and tram equipment.

1955 Bührer 0513
Right, top: *Bührer's 0513 featured a four-cylinder GM Opel diesel.*

1977 Hürlimann 5200
Right, bottom: *The Hürlimann 5200 was a 15/52-horsepower tractor with a two-range, five-speed gearbox. Owner: Jean Bronniman.*

1975 Hürlimann D-310

Hürlimann styling changed little from the mid-1950s to the mid-1970s, and this 25/85-horsepower four-cylinder diesel D-310 looks much like its 1950s counterpart. A strange feature of Hürlimanns from 1966 was the track rod above the axle working in two halves from a short central fulcrum.

1950s Vevey Model R tractors

A pair of forty-year-old Veveys still at work in Switzerland in 1997. The 1958 Vevey R at left was powered by a four-cylinder, 144-ci (2.36-liter) Perkins diesel; the firm also offered models with three-cylinder Perkins diesels. All had five forward gears until dual range boxes arrived in 1960. The Vevey factory still stands in Montreux, although it has not made tractors since 1962.

INDEX

ABOUT THE AUTHOR AND PHOTOGRAPHER

Nick Baldwin sits astride a Bamford rake pulled by his 1939 Schlüter DZM25 driven by George Grose on Baldwin's farm in Barrington, Somerset, Great Britain.

Nick Baldwin was brought up on an English farm during the days when the horse was replaced by the Fordson tractor. His first job was in the Land-Rover experimental department in the early 1960s. He became a freelance writer in the 1970s and has since written more than twenty books on tractors, cars, and trucks. Over the years, he has owned three International Titans, an International Junior, a Fordson Model F, a David Brown VAKI, and two Schlüter tractors. He lives on a farm in Somerset, Great Britain.

Andrew Morland was educated in Great Britain. He completed one year at Taunton College of Art in Somerset and then three years at London College of Printing studying photography. He has worked since graduation as a freelance photojournalist, traveling throughout Europe and North America. His work has been published in numerous magazines and books; related book titles include *Classic American Farm Tractors, Ford Tractors,* and *Fordson Tractors.* His interests include tractors, machinery, old motorbikes, and cars. He lives in a thatched cottage in Somerset, Great Britain, that was built in the 1680s. He is married and has one daughter.

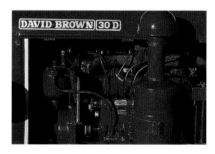